THE GREAT
HISPANIC HERITAGE

Salvador Dali

THE GREAT HISPANIC HERITAGE

THE GREAT
HISPANIC HERITAGE

Salvador Dali

Tim McNeese

CHELSEA HOUSE
PUBLISHERS

An imprint of Infobase Publishing

Salvador Dali

Chelsea House
An imprint of Infobase Publishing
132 West 31st Street
New York NY 10001

Library of Congress Cataloging-in-Publication Data

McNeese, Tim.
  Salvador Dali / Tim McNeese.
      p. cm. — (Great Hispanic heritage)
  Includes bibliographical references and index.
  ISBN 0-7910-8837-5 (hard cover)
  1. Dali, Salvador, 1904—Juvenile literature. 2. Artists—Spain—Biography—Juvenile literature. I. Title. II. Series.
  N7113.D3M39 2005
  709.2—dc22   2005025998

Chelsea House books are available at special discounts when purchased in bulk quantities for businesses, associations, institutions, or sales promotions. Please call our Special Sales Department in New York at (212) 967-8800 or (800) 322-8755.

You can find Chelsea House on the World Wide Web at http://www.chelseahouse.com

Text design by Terry Mallon
Cover design by Keith Trego

Printed in the United States of America

Bang EJB 10 9 8 7 6 5 4 3 2 1

This book is printed on acid-free paper.

All links and web addresses were checked and verified to be correct at the time of publication. Because of the dynamic nature of the web, some addresses and links may have changed since publication and may no longer be valid.

Table of Contents

Sur-realite

REVOLUTION AND CHANGE

The year was 1931, and calamitous change was blowing in on a strong wind across the political landscape of Spain. Seven years of harsh, autocratic rule at the hands of a Spanish general, Miguel Primo de Rivera, had finally come to an end in January 1930, and the fallout from the collapse of Rivera's dictatorial leadership was still taking place. After Rivera went into exile in Paris, a series of short-lived, "caretaker" governments had tried to restore order and direction to the lives of the Spanish people, but they all failed miserably. These governments were nearly as militaristic as Rivera's and had brought very little change. With each, though, there was the promise of general election—the last of which was in 1923. Each government promised; none delivered—that is, until that fateful spring of 1931.

On April 12, Spaniards, who were eager to lead their country

King Alfonso XIII ruled Spain from 1902 until he abdicated the throne in 1931, when the Second Republic came to power. This photo, taken on March 10, 1931, shows the king in a parlor of the Royal Palace in Madrid. Five weeks later, Alfonso XIII would flee Spain and take up residence in Paris.

out of chaos, went to the polls and voted in municipal elections. The political future of Spain was about to change. Through these disappointing years of leadership by the military, the Spanish Crown had remained intact. The king, Alfonso XIII, unable to challenge the power of the generals, had merely supported each dictator, and by doing so, had kept his royal crown and throne, even if it had meant he wielded no real power. Because of his personal weakness and failure to defy Spain's army, in 1931 the voters turned on their king. The new Spanish government would be one that would bend only to the will of the people. It would speak with a new voice; backed by the power of the voting public. The new system of power would rest on the shoulders of republicanism.

In the two days that followed this momentous election, the aristocracy collapsed. Taking his cue from the people (and from General Primo de Rivera) King Alfonso XIII, too, left his homeland and fled quietly to sanctuary in Paris, France. Alfonso's reign had ended, and "not even the leading monarchists were now prepared to speak a good word on his behalf."[1] With the way clear to lay the foundation for their new republic, on April 14, the Spanish people established the Second Republic in the long, winding history of Spain. The power of the king gave way to the power of the vote, and Spaniards who favored democracy celebrated this change joyously.

There were those who did not support these fledgling steps toward self-rule, however. The leaders of the Catholic Church, which had enjoyed the support and protection of the Spanish government for centuries, were not pleased. Three weeks after the founding of the new republic, Cardinal Segura y Sáenz, Archbishop of Toledo, launched a fiery letter of condemnation against the provisional government in Madrid, a government that was preparing to issue a broad list of political reforms that the Church opposed. The new, Republican government wanted to legalize divorce and prostitution. Its leaders wanted to create a fairer system of distributing land to the peasants. The new government also wanted to wrest control of public education from the

Catholic Church and secularize education. All these reforms angered the Church leadership. As for those who supported the new Spanish political revolution and the establishment of a new republic, they were angered by the Church's response. Some advocates of the new democracy expressed their anger at the Church's opposition by taking matters into their own hands. On May 11, angry groups in Madrid burned a Jesuit building and six convents. There were other, similar incidents across Spain. Changing political directions in Spain was proving difficult at best.

THE SURREALISTS

While these life-altering events were unfolding across the Iberian Peninsula, another group of Spaniards watched with keen interest. They were revolutionaries of another sort. They, too, were intent on redefining Spain's future. They were tired of the traditional ways—the old views of the world. They were ready to make a difference. They were not driven by a strong love of democracy, however. Many of them were driven by a different set of political theories and values. Nearly to a man, they were Communists, those driven by the left-wing ideology of nineteenth-century German philosopher Karl Marx. They believed the future of Spain rested in a full-fledged revolution of the working class, the proletariat, who suffered constantly under the yoke of oppression. Their oppressors were those who held the wealth—the bankers, financiers, businessmen, and factory owners. They wanted a revolution but not one to establish democracy. They wanted to create a classless Spain, where the workers held power and no one owned any property privately. In addition to Spain, revolution was occurring throughout 1930s Europe—in Germany, Italy, the newly formed Soviet Union—and it was coming from both the left and the right.

These were difficult years for Spain and for Europe. The 1930s were the years between the wars, World War I (1914–1918) and World War II (1939–1945). During this time,

The surrealist movement, which evolved from the concept of *sur-realite* ("beyond reality"), was developed in Paris in the early 1920s. Typical of a surrealist work, which placed an emphasis on fantastic and incongruous dream-like images, is Salvador Dali's *Paint-Maker's Plight*. This advertisement for S.C. Johnson & Son appeared in *Fortune* magazine in 1942 and was painted during a period when Dali was infatuated with eyes.

National Socialist leader Adolf Hitler wrested control from another struggling democracy, the German Weimar Republic. In Italy, rightist political extremists, the Fascists, under the leadership of the blustering Benito Mussolini, would oust their own king, just as the Republicans had done in Spain. Through this difficult decade of the 1930s, economic chaos would also redirect history. The industrial nations of Europe, as well as the United States, Canada, Australia, and Japan, would experience the effects of the Great Depression. It was a difficult time for many—years of war; years of economic problems, including severe unemployment and inflation.

In the midst of this era of political turmoil and economic upheaval, another revolution was taking place. This was not a political revolution, although many of its members were Communists. This revolution was led by a new group of artists, those who wanted to upset and bring change to the art world, just as Republicans on one hand and Communists on the other sought to bring change to Spain, Germany, and other European states. This new artistic movement was known as surrealism.

The movement had begun during the early 1920s, in Paris, the artistic capital of modern art. The name was first created by writers, poets, and intellectuals in the movement who took the concept *sur-realite*, which translates as "beyond reality," and applied it to their new view of the world around them. They were soon eagerly joined by others—painters, sculptors, photographers—who wanted to portray surrealism in their art and their pictures. Just as the political extremists of this fertile period of transformation were seeking radical change, so also were the surrealists interested in bringing about a change in how they viewed the world of reality. The surrealists were bored with the real world, with the normal means of expression. They sought to break all rules, to take their imaginations to new places. They believed strongly in the power of dreams, of the unexplored corners of the human mind and the unconscious. To many of those on the outside, the surrealists were strange, indeed. They defied convention; sought the strange; engaged in what appeared to be eccentric, weird behaviors; made films that shocked their viewers; wrote self-conscious, disturbed essays, novels, and poetry; and covered their canvases with everything from floating donkeys to melting clocks. And among those who set the style, the direction, the ideology,

HOW DALI AND THE SURREALISTS TURNED THE WORLD UPSIDE DOWN

Who and what were the surrealists? When Dali was painting such works as *Apparatus and Hand*, the artistic and philosophical movement in art and literature was just beginning. The word *surreal*, which means "more than real" or even "better than real,"* was coined by the creators of surrealism. This bizarre, symbolic approach to art was created and defined in 1924 by André Breton, who would become the recognized leader of the movement.

That year, Breton would organize the publication of the first *Surrealist Manifesto*, which described the goals and ideas of the surrealists. (To further his point, Breton had himself pictured in the *Manifesto* wearing a suit and a crown of thorns.) Once established, the movement began to expand, driven by a self-conscious approach to creative thought and artistic expression. From 1925 and over the following decade or so, surrealism was the *cause célèbre*, the motivation for a group of artists and writers. (Dali, as it turns out, was both.) A notable exhibition of surrealist paintings was held in 1925, in Paris; it included paintings by such established surrealist artists as the German Max Ernst and Joan Miró, whom Breton referred to as "the most surrealist of all."** (Even though Dali joined the surrealist movement in its early stages, because of his age, he became one of the artists of a second, younger generation of surrealists.)

At the center of surrealism was a dramatic form of liberation of the arts, including the canvas, the film screen, and the printed page. Surrealists were interested in the "interaction between the phenomena of the objective, external world and the interior workings of the individual and, ultimately, the reputation of the surrealists was a Spaniard, a conflicted genius whose father was an atheist and whose mother was a devout Catholic—Salvador Dali.

mind."*** Taking cues from Sigmund Freud's studies of the human psyche, the surrealists tried to depict in their art "life as lived in the human mind."† As painters, they strove to use their art to depict "the unconscious, dreams, trance states, poetic thoughts, memories, evocations, and psychological or psychopathological associations."†† It was the landscape of the mind they were seeking. The surrealists constantly explored the world of dreams. Their movement swept through Paris during the 1920s and would remain an important international art movement for the next three decades.

Surprisingly, this avant-garde artistic movement was created, in part, as a challenge to other, earlier modern art movements, including fauvism. Although the fauvists, led by the French painter Henri Matisse, had at first shocked the art world at the beginning of the twentieth century with their bright colors and light subject matter, in time, the movement won many admirers who came to find the fauvist works acceptable, even comforting, and certainly hopeful. Matisse himself once said that "a good painting should be just as soothing as 'a good armchair.'"††† That view of art was completely unacceptable to the surrealists, however. Their primary goal was to shock viewers and readers. They wanted their audience not only to look at their works, but also to have strong feelings, including negative reactions, toward the artists' unsettling subject matter.

　* Robert Anderson, *Salvador Dali* (Danbury, Conn.: Franklin Watts, 2002), 18.
　** Ibid.
　*** Kenneth Wach, *Salvador Dali: Masterpieces from the Collection of the Salvador Dali Museum* (New York: Harry N. Abrams, 1996), 14.
　† Ibid.
　†† Ibid.
　††† Anderson, *Salvador Dali*, 19.

The Trauma

THE MOST SIGNIFICANT EVENT

He was named after his father and his great-grandfather: Salvador, the Savior. Salvador Dali was born on May 11, 1904, at his parents' home in Figueres, Spain. The birth took place at 8:45 in the morning, an event that Dali himself would one day describe as "the most significant event" of his life. As an adult, Dali claimed to remember being born, stating he suffered "the horrible traumatism of birth."[2] His birthday would mark, then, the beginning of a life motivated by fantasy.

He was christened on May 20 in the local parish church of St. Peter. His full name was Salvador Felipe Jacinto Dali i Domenech. (Felipe is the male version of his mother's name, and he was given the name "Jacinto" in honor of one of his uncles.) For his parents, the birth of this son was not their first. Three years earlier, Dali's mother, Felipa Domenech Ferres, had given birth to another son, whom they also named Salvador. But at the age of 22 months,

14

Figueres, which is located near the Pyrenees Mountains of north-eastern Spain, is the birthplace of Salvador Dali. In 1926, Dali painted *Woman at the Window at Figueres*, which portrays his sister Ana Maria sewing on a balcony overlooking their hometown.

the Dalis' firstborn died. With the birth of their second "Salvador" just a year following the death of their firstborn, the Dalis were prepared to lavish a lifetime of love on their new-born son. In doing so, their overprotective, doting love proba-bly helped produce a young child who would, at an early age, enjoy being the center of attention and be prone to excessive behavior. As for Dali himself, how acutely he felt the struggle represented by his parents' loss is not certain. As an adult, the artist frequently acted out in bizarre ways, drawing almost constant attention to himself. In one of his writings, he explained his behavior by alluding to his brother: "All the eccentricities that I commit, I do because I wish to prove to myself that I am not the dead brother, but the living one."[3]

The Dalis were a highly respected couple in Figueres. Dali's father, Salvador Dali Cusi, was a local Catalonian notary public, one of only five in the region. He was also a well-respected lawyer who had received his law degree in 1893. His wife, Felipa, was described as "a demure and pretty Barcelona girl two years younger than [her husband]."[4] Her family was equally respected in the business world of Barcelona, where her father was a haberdasher (merchant of men's clothing). The parents of Salvador Dali met while vacationing in the small village of Cabrils. Following a short courtship, Salvador and Felipa were married on December 29, 1900, in Barcelona, in the Church of Nuestra Denora de la Merced. Within a few weeks of their marriage, Felipa was pregnant.

The place of Salvador Dali's birth, Figueres, was a typical Spanish town, its population numbering 11,000. (Today, Figueres is home to more than 30,000 inhabitants.) The town lay near the "beautiful and fertile Upper Empordá plain"[5] and served as the region's capital. The northern Spanish town is a mere 15 miles from the southern border of France, near the foothills of the Pyrenees Mountains. The region of Figueres is known as the Empordá, through which flow the dual rivers of the Tech (in France) and El Ter (in Spain). It has also been a fluid region of occupation, as various ethnic groups—successive waves of ancient Phoenicians, Greeks, and Romans, followed by Arab invaders—have claimed Empordá as their own. The landscape is legendary, finding its place in myths and stories of King Arthur, Charlemagne, and the Saracens. For the adult Dali, the region remained infused in his mind's eye and provided "the background of his mature works."[6]

The Dalis lived in an apartment in Figueres—Carrer Monturiol 20—that still stands. Salvador Dali was raised in a home in which his parents lavished him with attention. The apartment would be the family home until 1912. It was here that young Salvador formed some of his early childhood memories. The apartment was located on the building's first floor and looked out over a splendid garden owned by a local aristocrat. Along the apartment's exterior, a lengthy *galleria*, or balcony, faced the garden. The garden was lined with great chestnut trees with branches that nearly reached the balcony itself, providing anyone on the balcony with at least some privacy. Although Dali does not mention the apartment in his writings, his younger sister, Ana Maria, remembered the balcony was "embellished with pots of lilies and sweet-smelling spikenard"[7] (the flower would become the adult Dali's favorite). Ana Maria also had fond memories of her mother, Felipa, who was a bird lover and kept an aviary filled with canaries and doves at one end of the balcony.

A SPOILED CHILD

Of his two parents, young Salvador was probably pampered more by his mother than his father. In his later years, he remembered his mother, a devout Roman Catholic, with warmth and affection. He would describe her as "the honey in the family."[8] A day never passed without the Dalis giving their son nearly everything he wanted, helping create in young Salvador a lifelong spirit of self-indulgence and selfishness. To put their toddler son to sleep, the Dalis often sang to him their vast repertoire of traditional Catalan lullabies and folksongs. According to the adult Dali, he recalled being awakened each morning by his mother, who would "look lovingly in his eyes" and ask him: "Sweet heart, what do you want? Sweet heart, what do you desire?"[9]

Perhaps the Dalis embellished their son's wants and needs because they had lost one son already. Perhaps they were trying to make young Salvador's seemingly constant battle with nosebleeds and angina a bit more bearable. They, as well as other relatives, did lavish attention on him, however. One day an uncle gave him a special present: the costume of a king, which Salvador eagerly adorned. As he later described himself, he was "the absolute monarch of the house."[10]

For the first four years of his life, Salvador Dali was an only child. He became a young boy who was constantly throwing temper tantrums. Much of this behavior seemed to stem from his desire to receive even more attention than he was already getting. He was especially prone to tantrums at Christmas. He loved receiving presents so much that he became impatient for the arrival of the special holiday. According to his sister, during family visits to Barcelona, he "got so worked up he never stopped crying and raging."[11] At Christmas, his parents and other family members "gave him so many presents that he used

BEING HISPANIC

MEMORIES OF CATALONIA AND BARCELONA

One of the most profound influences on Salvador Dali's artistic style was his place of birth: Spain's Catalonia (also spelled "Catalunya") region, which is situated in the farthest, northeast corner of the Iberian Peninsula. The region extends to the French border, as well as to the tiny state of Andorra in the eastern Pyrenees Mountains. Surrounded by mountains and bordered by the Mediterranean Sea, Catalonia has been able, for centuries, to keep itself separated from the rest of the country, allowing its people to develop an independent and proud identity. Its people even have their own language—Catalan—which is set apart from Castilian Spanish, the language spoken by most Spaniards. Salvador Dali certainly felt strongly about his Catalonian roots.

Catalonia's landscapes and topography often inspired Dali's art. The region's countryside includes a rambling, rugged plain set against a long coastline strewn with mammoth rock formations. Its rock-littered beaches are lapped by the warm waters of the Mediterranean. As Dali grew up, he and his family visited the coast and its great rock formations frequently, spending summer vacations there and even weekends during the rest of the year.

Throughout their independent history, the Catalonians developed a distinct culture, and, historically, they have been fiercely supportive of to go quite berserk."[12] His love of presents never left him, even as a selfish and overindulged adult. Throughout his life, though, Dali rarely gave presents to others.

His childhood behavior became legendary:

> From the day he came into the world his every whim was catered to, and he quickly learnt that, by exercising . . . his "terrible temper," he could invariably bend his parents to his

the fine arts, including painting, architecture, literature, and music. For hundreds of years, the people of this region have been able to pursue their love of the arts. The capital city of Catalonia, Barcelona is the center of the region's art and literature. Today, the city remains second only to Madrid as the artistic center of Spain. For the Catalonians, their city is number one. During Dali's early years, Barcelona was home to some of the region's most famous and popular artists, including the painters Pablo Picasso and Joan Miró. It is the site of one of the most interesting and unique cathedrals ever constructed, the magnificent *Sagrada Familia* (Holy Family Church), which was designed by the great Spanish architect Antonio Gaudi.

The elder Salvador frequently took his son on visits to Barcelona. The city was a prosperous urban center, filled with excitement. There were many new buildings and city parks, and Dali was able to see the Sagrada Familia. According to Dali, the church's strange architecture—its "melting" stone masonry—would later inspire some of his artistic masterpieces. His father frequented a local café, *Els Quatre Gats* ("The Four Cats"), one of Barcelona's most popular haunts for writers, intellectuals, and artists, including Picasso, who was known to be a regular.

The adult Salvador Dali lived in many different places, including several countries, but he never forgot his homeland. Catalonia remained in his memory throughout his life, and its inspiring landscapes found their place in Dali's art. The region also instilled in the eccentric, free-thinking painter a love of artistic stimulation and expression.

will . . . the family discovered that the only way to keep Salvador quiet was never to deny him what he wanted but, rather, to coax him surreptitiously into demanding something more reasonable.[13]

To keep young Salvador entertained, his parents often took him to the cinema, which he greatly loved. There were movies featuring Charlie Chaplin and French-born Max Linder, one of film's earliest comic stars. The adult Dali remembered two films specifically: a documentary on the Russo-Japanese War and *The Enamoured Student*. Film became a lifelong obsession of Dali's.

At age four, young Salvador would no longer be the only child in the Dali household. His mother gave birth to a daughter, Ana Maria. How the arrival of a sibling changed life for Dali is not clear. He never writes about what he thought of his newly arrived sister, although he claims to have kicked her in the head when she was two years old. Of course, whether he actually kicked Ana Maria or not is speculation, but it is likely that a child as spoiled and self-centered as young Dali probably wanted to do just that. He did act out in other ways, however. According to the adult Dali, he claims to have wet his bed regularly until the age of eight, not because he could not help himself, but "for the sheer fun of it."[14] In his autobiography, Dali claims, when he was only five years old, he pushed a younger child off of a bridge from a height of 15 feet. He also claims to have gleefully hidden his excrement around the family apartment, so his parents would have to search for it. Again, Dali may have claimed more than he actually did as a youth.

For all his personal selfishness and outrageous behavior as a young man, though, Dali was also capable of tenderness and sensitivity, as well as personal fear. (He developed lifelong phobias at an early age; for example, he was petrified of grasshoppers.) At the age of five, he found a bat with a broken wing. He took the bat into the family laundry house and placed it in a bucket so he could nurse it to recovery. He even placed "a glow worm beside it so as to create a kind of shrine."[15] As the days passed, young Salvador became affectionate toward the bat and sometimes kissed it on the forehead. Unfortunately, his tender efforts to save the bat failed when a colony of ants invaded the bat's pail and ate the suffering creature alive, which greatly upset Dali.

In these early years, Dali was also coming to value solitude. As much as he enjoyed attention from his parents, as well as other family members, including aunts and uncles, and a nurse named Lucia Moncanut, he found comfort in being alone. He later wrote how as a teenager he would go to the family laundry room and spend time by himself. The room included a large cement basin, which young Dali would fill with water, then sit in for hours at a time. Here he would contemplate and imagine to his heart's content, away from others, away from their attentions.

EARLY SCHOOL DAYS

At age four, about the time his sister was born, Salvador was sent to school. He attended a public institution, although his father had enough money to send him to private school. The Figueres Municipal Primary School would occupy young Dali for the next two years. The old school master was Señor Esteban Trayter Colomer, whom Salvador remembered for drilling into him such lessons as "God does not exist" and "Religion was something for women."[16] Again, whether Dali's memories are accurate is unknown. From this earliest beginning of his education, Dali appears to have been a poorly motivated, distracted, and disinterested student. It was difficult to teach him anything. He did not pay attention, often staring off at the walls or ceiling, endlessly focusing on "stains on the classroom ceiling"[17] made by a leaky roof. In the rusty, water-marked ceiling panels, young Dali could see images, shapes, and other manner of fantasy. Such behavior helped to fuel his acute imagination.

At this early age, Dali did not indulge in the type of eccentric behavior that became part of his character in secondary school. He did remember clearly that he knew at the school how much better off his family was financially than the families of his classmates. His affectionate mother dressed him in nice, expensive clothes, whereas most of the other boys came to school in cheaper clothing. In his writings, Dali claims that this awareness of being better dressed than the other students only encouraged his "natural tendencies to megalomania."[18]

Although Dali did not appear to enjoy his studies at the primary school, he did have clear memories of Señor Trayter, whose appearance was memorable. A school photograph shows that, although the 50-ish teacher's hair was cut short, he sported a long beard, which he kept in two great strands that extended down to his waist. Dali also recalled visiting Trayter's home (The Trayters lived near the Dalis.) There, he found his school master's den "a magic cave", featuring a towering bookcase filled with many volumes. Trayter also had a collection of odd items that fascinated young Salvador: a large rosary he had bought in Jerusalem; a statue of a devil, whose arm moved up and down, carrying a pitchfork; and a dead frog hanging on a string, which Trayter used to predict the weather. The greatest novelty for young Dali, however, was Trayter's French stereoscope, a turn-of-the-century form of slide projector. The stereoscope was a marvel to Salvador:

> I have never been able to determine or reconstruct in my mind exactly what it was like. As I remember it one saw everything as if at the bottom of and through a very limpid and stereoscopic water, which became successively and continually coloured with the most varied iridescences . . . It was in this marvelous theatre of Senor Trayter that I saw the images which were to stir me most deeply for the rest of my life.[19]

In his writings, Dali clearly remembered Trayter's pictures. Among the collection, the adult Dali recalled a "series of views

Salvador Dali, pictured here in 1930, had the fortune of being surrounded by several creative people during his youth. One of the most prominent was Ramon Pichot, who introduced the young artist to modern art while the Dali family spent their summers at the seaside village of Cadaques.

of snow-bound Russian landscapes studded with cupolas, and, among these, by a sequence of a pretty little Russian girl in a sledge, enveloped in white furs."[20] Dali would eventually marry a young Russian woman. He became convinced that the girl in Trayter's stereographic slide show was his wife, Gala.

During these early school years for Salvador Dali, his family frequently spent weekends and long summers vacationing outside Figueres, often visiting the seaside village of Cadaques. These excursions to the beach helped form important memories for Dali, as the family often spent their days with family and friends, especially the Pichot family. The family's father, Josep "Pepito" Pichot Girones, was an old friend of Dali's father, the two men having met as students at the Instituto in Barcelona. (Young Dali remembered the Pichot house, a rambling mansion set in the heart of Barcelona's Garrigal Quarter, as "one of the most marvelous places of my childhood.")[21] During these seaside visits, young Salvador and his sister, Ana Maria, spent much of their time frolicking along the beaches, examining the marine life in dozens of rock and tide pools. Some of his father's friends set up their easels along the beaches, and painted landscapes of local rock formations and the gently breaking sea waters of the Mediterranean.

The Dalis usually spent their time staying at the Pichots' seaside home, Es Sortell. Eventually, they built a summer vacation house of their own not far from the Pichots. As for young Dali, he loved the beachside and the times his family spent with the Pichots and their friends, many of whom were painters, musicians, and nonconformists. The boy took in the sights of the romantic local village, the great rock formations along the beach, the music, the art, and the adults conversing on an endless litany of topics. As for the local, massive rock formations along the beach, Dali took inspiration from them and used them in his adult paintings. Many of the beachside formations had names corresponding with their general appearance and shape—"The Eagle," "The Monk," "The Rhinoceros," and "The Dead Woman." These rocks eventually became part of Dali's "mental landscape"[22] and throughout his life, he would use these images in his art.

The Young Artist

STUDENT AND TEACHER

After two years in primary school, young Salvador was enrolled in Immaculate Conception School, a Catholic institution run by the Christian Brothers, a teaching order established in France in the 1700s. The order had been banned from teaching in France, pushed out by a rival Catholic order, the Jesuits. Thus, they had several schools in Spain. In 1910, the year of Dali's enrollment, the school in Figueres had only been open for a year.

Although Dali's father was an atheist, he decided to place his son in the Christian Brothers' school because they taught all their lessons in French and he wanted Salvador to become fluent in the language. During the six years young Dali attended the school, he did learn to speak French fluently, even though he retained a heavy Catalan accent. As for the written language, its "unphonetic spelling was beyond him,"[23] and he was never able to write French with any accuracy.

As with his earlier school experience, young Salvador was not a good student. He was highly intelligent but easily distracted and bored. He did not concentrate well on his studies and daydreamed often, and because he was bored, he frequently doodled on his schoolwork. Although his interest in most subjects was minimal, one subject probably did encourage his personal talent—art class. The records of the Immaculate Conception school do not explain exactly what classes a student such as Dali might have taken as a young child, but it is known from his own writings that young Salvador did appreciate at least one teacher—his art instructor. He wrote in his early 20s in praise of that instructor, whose name remains unknown. According to Dali, this teacher would often "issue to his pupils . . . simple drawings done himself with a ruler, and then require them to block them in carefully with watercolours."[24] Dali recalled a singular piece of "common sense" advice from his art teacher: "To paint them well, to paint well in general, consists in not going over the line."[25] As an adult artist, much of Salvador Dali's work was precise and attentive to extremely small details. He may have owed some of his "technical" skill to his teacher at Immaculate Conception.

In 1912, at the end of Dali's second year at Immaculate Conception, the family moved to another apartment, Carrer Monturiol 24. The family's new home was on the top floor of a brand-new building, designed by one of Figueres' leading architects. Gone was the family's romantic balcony with its birds and spikenard and its splendid gardens below. Although Salvador never mentions the move in his writings, Ana Maria does, describing the move as a "loss of her childhood paradise."[26] The more spacious and luxurious apartment was fitting for the prosperous Dali family. It was here that young Salvador would first paint, capturing the panoramic sweep of the townscape from the apartment's rooftop. It was in the building's laundry room that Dali would sit in seclusion in the cement tub. In that rooftop washroom, he set up his first artist studio. Young Dali came to love the new apartment's rooftop terrace, where he strutted around in a king's costume, dressed out in "the ermine cape, crown and sceptre that had been given to him by one of his uncles in Barcelona."[27]

A FLAIR FOR THE DRAMATIC

Over the next few years, Dali continued attending classes at Immaculate Conception. By 1916, he was advanced to secondary school, where he began his work on a six-year state baccalaureate course of study. From 1916 through 1921, Salvador attended the Figueres Institute and the Academy of the Marist Order. During these years, he began to develop a tendency for outrageous public behavior. He became more and more bizarre and enjoyed exhibitionism. It would become a lifelong practice:

> He extracted money from his parents and sold it to his fellow pupils for half its value. His outbursts of aggression became more frequent and vicious, attacks being perpetrated on any pupil who looked sufficiently incapable of resistance . . . By the age of 16 he had discovered the attention which he could command by flinging himself down flights of stairs.[28]

To get attention, he also began wearing his mother's face powder, to give himself the look of the unconventional "Bohemian artist." He wore heavy sideburns and let his thick black hair grow down past his shoulders. He paraded around in fashionable cloaks and capes, and began carrying a walking stick. Years later, even as an adult, he continued some of these outrageous behaviors.

Although school still failed to inspire him, Salvador was becoming more interested in art. He spent many hours in his washroom studio. Among his artist's belongings, young Dali had a complete, multivolume set of *Gowans' Art Books*, which were first published in 1905, and were well-known at the time as a rich, visual resource of art history. Each book (there would eventually be 52 volumes) contained 60 black-and-white pictures of some of the greatest works of art in European history. Dali later wrote about the importance the Gowans books had on him:

> These little monographs which my father had so prematurely given me as a present produced an effect on me that was one of the most decisive in my life. I came to know by heart all those pictures of the history of art, which have been familiar to me since my earliest childhood, for I would spend entire days contemplating them.[29]

These art books provided Dali's first inspiration to paint. Young Salvador's earliest known paintings were probably produced when he was 10 or 11 years old, following the family's move to Monturiol 24. They were five small, undated landscapes, painted on cardboard. The scenes include green fields; a scattering of buildings; a massive factory chimney; a snow-covered mountain; fields of poppies; and a Romanesque church, Saint Mary of Vilabertran, "whose twelfth-century, three storied bell tower was visible from Dali's classroom at the Christian Brothers."[30]

EL MOLI DE LA TORRE

Dali's father was instrumental in encouraging his son's artistic talents. He purchased the Gowans series for Salvador and encouraged his son to spend more time with the Pichot family, whose members were deeply involved and influential in the various arts, including impressionist painting. At age 12, young Dali was spending his summer vacations with the family of Ramon Pichot at their estate house, El Moli de la Torre, *the Tower Mill*, situated just outside the village of Figueres.

The Pichots were from Barcelona, where they kept their main residence, but spent time in Figueres and in Cadaques, at their summer house. Ramon Pichot—the brother of Josep—painted in the manner of the impressionists and was friends with some of the most important Spanish artists, including

Ramon Pichot's impressionist works, such as *Portrait of Francisco de Asis Cambo Batile*, helped inspire Salvador Dali during his formative years. When he visited the Pichot seaside home in Cadaques, the young Dali would often study Pichot's paintings, which were hung throughout the house.

the great Picasso, who was already beginning to experiment with cubism, and André Derain, one of the early radical painters to produce works as a fauvist. It was probably through Ramon that Dali was first seriously introduced to the world of art, although Dali's father was friends with various artists, as well.

The entire household of Ramon Pichot seemed gifted in the arts. Among his children, Ricard was an accomplished

(*continued on page 32*)

AN INTRODUCTION TO PICASSO

Life in the midst of the Pichot family and their friends "must have been thrilling as Salvador advanced from childhood to adolescence."* Within this swirl of art, nature, the sea, friends, and adolescent adventure, Dali may have been introduced to one of the greatest twentieth-century Spanish artists—Pablo Picasso.

By the early twentieth century, Pablo Picasso was the most famous Spanish painter in Europe. Born in 1881, in the small town of Malaga on the southern coast of the Andalusia region, Picasso had begun his artistic career as a young man. In 1900, at the age of 19, he had moved to Paris, the center of early-twentieth-century European art. There, he was caught up in the whirlwind of the rapidly changing world of modern art. Through the following decade, his artistic style underwent many changes, as he experimented with impressionism, fauvism, and, by 1909, the innovative style that he helped create, cubism.

In the summer of 1910, when Salvador was only 6 years old, 29-year-old Picasso, already a recognized name in the world of modern art, visited the Pichots at Es Sortell. Picasso was a friend of Ramon Pichot, Josep Pichot Girones' brother. (Ramon was nine years older than Picasso.) At the time, Picasso was living with one of his many lovers, a young woman named Fernande Olivier. Picasso painted some of his important works while in Cadaques, using the local landscapes as his inspiration. Dali had no immediate memory of Picasso's stay with the Pichot family that summer; however, he was, after all, only six years old. It is possible that Dali's father may have met Picasso even earlier than 1910. Ramon Pichot and Picasso had become friends by the late 1890s, and the elder Salvador may have been introduced through Ramon to Picasso at the Pichot family apartment or at a café the three men were known to frequent, Barcelona's Els Quatre Gats.

Although the two young men were more than 20 years apart in age, as Spanish artists, they were both inspired by earlier Spanish painters. Picasso was a great admirer of such Spanish artists as Velázquez, Zurbarán, Goya, and, especially, El Greco. Equally, young Salvador Dali found inspiration in these painters from earlier centuries. Both artists attended the Royal Academy of San Fernando, in Madrid. Dali would, at least during the early 1920s, embrace Picasso's cubism as his artistic style. The parallel lives of these two innovators in Spanish art crossed repeatedly.

The first documented meeting between the two painters took place in 1926, during Dali's first visit to Paris, the center of modern art during the 1920s. When he entered Picasso's studio, Dali spoke to the great, middle-aged Picasso: "I have visited you before going to the Louvre."** (The Louvre is one of Europe's greatest repositories of art, a must-see for anyone visiting Paris for the first time.) Picasso's response: "You were not wrong."***

Although the earlier encounter—if there was one at all in 1910—between Dali and Picasso was not in itself important, the two men would become two of the most recognized Spanish artists. Dali, of course, understood this, and gave a speech in 1951, which he titled, "Picasso and I." In that speech, Salvador spoke of the similarities between the two men, describing them both as "Spanish" and "geniuses," then he added: "As always, Spain has the honour of producing the greatest contrasts, this time in the persons of the two most antagonic artists of modern painting: Picasso and myself, your humble servant."†

* Ian Gibson, *The Shameful Life of Salvador Dali* (New York: W.W. Norton, 1997), 73.

** Robert Anderson, *Salvador Dali* (Danbury, Conn.: Franklin Watts, 2002), 12.

*** Robert Goff, *The Essential Salvador Dali* (New York: Harry N. Abrams, 1998), 36.

† Gibson, *The Shameful Life of Salvador Dali*, 520.

(*continued from page 29*)

cellist whose teacher was the famed Pablo Casals, and his brother, Luis, was a concert violinist. A sister, Maria, was famous as a popular Spanish opera singer. Another sister, Mercedes, was the wife of the well-known literary figure Eduardo Marquina. It was in the midst of this pantheon of talent that Dali "began to develop the wide reading, diverse cultural pursuits, and broad artistic interests that mark his maturity."[31]

That first summer would mark Dali's emergence not only into the world of art but also into that of adolescence. At El Moli de la Torre, he was introduced to the 16-year-old adopted daughter of Pepito Pichot, whose "blossoming body rivets his attention."[32] Despite the allure of the enticing Julia, young Dali greatly admired and was intrigued by the artistic work of Ramon Pichot. The Spanish artist's styles included an early variety of French impressionism. Dali later compared some of Pichot's earlier works to the innovative French painter and lithographic designer Toulouse-Lautrec. Dali, however, was most impressed with the paintings on which Ramon was working in more recent years: "[The] paintings that filled me with the greatest wonder were the most recent ones, in which deliquescent impressionism ended in certain canvases by frankly adopting in an almost uniform manner the *pointilliste* formula."[33] Ramon's paintings were hung throughout the Pichot house, especially the dining room, and young Salvador studied them constantly.

Guidance and inspiration visited Dali during his summers at "The Tower Mill" and through his connections with the Pichot family. He began to paint seriously. He was introduced to one of the region's most important and talented artists and engravers, Juan Núñez Fernández, with whom Dali studied drawing and printmaking. Núñez was one of the respected instructors at the Municipal School of Drawing in Figueres, and was trained at the Royal Academy of San Fernando in Madrid, the most prestigious art school in Spain. More than a century earlier, the great Spanish painter Goya had served as

During the early 1920s, Salvador Dali embraced cubism, a movement that was introduced to the artistic world by Pablo Picasso (pictured here) and Georges Braque. Picasso and Dali were both friends of the Pichots and often visited the family's seaside house in Cadaques, which served as inspiration to both men throughout their careers.

the Academy's director, and, in more recent decades, Pablo Picasso had studied art there.

A BUDDING ARTIST

Dali honed his talents under Núñez, who served as Dali's art teacher for six years, at the Municipal School and at the

Instituto. Salvador admired his instructor and, writing in later years, admitted a debt to the older maestro in helping him develop his abilities with brush and paint:

> He was truly devoured by an authentic passion for the Fine Arts. From the beginning he singled me out among the hundred students in the class, and invited me to his house, where he would explain to me the "savage strokes" . . . of an original engraving by Rembrandt . . . I would always come away from Senor Nunez's home stimulated to the highest degree, my cheeks flushed with the greatest artistic ambitions.[34]

Perhaps no one had a more profound impact on young Salvador's art than his teacher, Señor Núñez. While studying with Núñez, Dali's talents began to take their form and, at age 13, Salvador received a prize certificate from the Municipal School of Drawing.

He was also working with oils. In 1917, when he was 13, Dali painted his *View of Cadaques with Shadow of Mount Pani*. Already, at a young age, Salvador was showing an extreme level of sophistication in his painting. The painting's composition balances the shadowy, dark greens of a grove of umbrella pines on the right and foreground, with brighter yellowish and pinkish tones of a muted setting sun and the glowering lights of the village of Cadaques ringing its blue-tinted bay.

Although this painting was similar to those of nearly every other impressionist painter at the time, the 13-year-old Dali was also creating innovative art, as well. On one painting, he used only three colors, "which he squeezed direct from the tube."[35] But then, he began experimenting with the work:

> Dali painted a pile of cherries using a worm-eaten door as a support. Reality and illusion then cross-migrated. He planted the stems of the real cherries, which he was using as a model, in the wet paint then, using a hairpin, he picked the worms out of the door and transplanted them to the holes made in the real

cherries. When Senor [Pichot] saw this he muttered "That shows genius."[36]

Not only did the Pichot family provide young Dali with support in his early days as a budding artist but so did his father. The elder Salvador posted his son's drawings and other artwork throughout the family home. In the fall of 1916, Dali's father managed to get his son accepted into art school, the Figueres Instituto, where he studied under Señor Núñez. Dali's first year of study at the Instituto went exceedingly well, and he passed his first-year exams with high marks in May 1917.

Under Nunez's tutelage, Dali produced another oil painting, *Port of Cadaques (Night)*, which he painted between 1918 and 1919. Again, as with his other works of this period, the painting is an impressionist study, this one featuring dark, somber colors depicting a ship's bow in the darkened harbor, flanked by smaller boats on its starboard, while, in the distance, the village hugs the twilight shoreline on the ship's port. Young Dali has chosen to make his artistic statements with bold strokes, including broad, squiggly reflections of the town's buildings in the shimmering night waters. He applied his colors directly from the paint tubes. The result is a heavy-handed working of the canvas, with the buildings appearing as ephemeral as the nature of the water itself. With its paints and its textures, Dali's work is experimental, as the color is laid on the canvas thickly and freely, revealing his understanding of the impasto technique popular during this period of painting. There would be other, similarly painted oils produced by Dali between 1918 and 1919, including landscapes set in and around Cadaques: *Hort del Llane*, *Portdogue*, and *View of Portdogue (Port Alguer)*, as well as a light, fauvist self-portrait, cast in stark shades of red, of Dali at his easel.

The young artist was busying himself with other talents. Living among the literary Pichots, Dali also began writing, finding special interest in stories and personal journal entries. And he took his artwork public. In 1918, at a local Figueres art show, young Dali showed two oil paintings. He was studying more and more art, not only from the pages of the Gowans volumes but modern art movements, including the developing cubism of Pablo Picasso and others. The following year, he exhibited with the Sociedad de Conciertos, a local art group in Figueres. He sold two of his paintings, probably the first purchases of his early years. In a local newspaper, the *Empordia Federal*, Salvador's painting was praised:

> Dali Domenech, a man who can feel the light . . . is already one of those artists who will cause a great sensation . . . one of those who will produce great pictures . . . We welcome this new artist and express our belief that at some point in the future our humble words will prove to be prophetic.[37]

Young Dali was only 15. His studies were improving his art, but he was coming to understand more and more about the rigors of creativity. In a letter he sent to an uncle that summer, young Salvador admitted: "I'm growing more and more aware all the time of the difficulty of art; but I'm also growing to enjoy it and love it increasingly."[38]

That same year—1919—Dali's artistic and literary interests were both flowering. He wrote for the student publication, *Studium*, where he penned a poem and several prose pieces, including essays on his favorite artists, such as the Spanish masters El Greco, Velázquez, and Goya, as well as Italian masters of the High Renaissance, Michelangelo and Leonardo Da Vinci. Such writings were all part of Dali's ever increasing confidence in himself as a painter, a modern artist in the making. In a diary entry from 1919, he predicted of himself: "I'll be a genius, and the world will admire me."[39]

AN ARTISTIC FUTURE

Over the next two years, Dali continued to write, draw, and paint. By age 17, he was producing several oils a year, largely landscapes, all fitting within the accepted, experimental parameters of early-1920s modern art. In 1921, Dali's father managed to have his son enrolled in the Royal Academy of San Fernando in Madrid. (As for Dali's secondary school experiences, he had been expelled by then.) In the midst of these plans for Dali's artistic training, however, personal tragedy struck.

His mother died that year of uterine cancer. She died somewhat abruptly, and her death was a shock to her family and friends. Felipa Domenech was only 47 years old. For Dali, now in his late teens, the blow was crushing. He wrote of his departed mother: "She adored me with a love so whole and so proud that she could not be wrong."[40] At first, his reaction to the death caused him to act as though it had happened to him—that her death was a personal affront, an insult. In time, he began to work out a strategy of "revenge": "With my teeth clenched with weeping, I swore to myself that I would snatch my mother from the death and destiny with the swords of light that some day would savagely gleam around my glorious name!"[41] Out of his mother's death, 17-year-old Salvador Dali was determined to gain fame through his art.

Finding His Art

NEW SCHOOL, NEW FRIENDS

Salvador Dali probably never fully recovered from the death of his mother. This tragic personal event traumatized him dramatically. He was further antagonized when his father married his mother's sister soon afterward. As for his art, although much of his earlier work had focused on simple, straightforward portraits of family, friends, and himself, he began to paint subjects that appeared darker, "making images that reflect his tormented soul."[42] Before he arrived at the Royal Academy of San Fernando to take up his artistic studies, he faced yet another personal loss: Pepito Pichot, his family's longtime friend, also died.

When Dali arrived at the prestigious Madrid school in September 1921, he proved himself an exemplary student—at first. Although he only remained at the school for a year, during that time period, he changed dramatically. He lived in housing known as the Residencia de Estudiantes, where he came into contact with other

One of Dali's closest friends while he was a student at the Royal Academy of San Fernando in Madrid was the poet Federico Garcia Lorca. During the Spanish Civil War, Lorca's work was banned by Fascist leader Francisco Franco, and he was later executed in 1936 due to his support of the deposed Republican government.

students, several of whom were talented and exceptional, including Federico Garcia Lorca, José Bello, Pedro Garfias, and Luis Buñuel, who became one of Dali's closest friends while he attended the art school in Madrid. Buñuel would later become a famous surrealist filmmaker. (Dali would paint an oil portrait of his friend Luis in 1924.) As for Lorca, he, too, became a close associate of Dali's for many years following their time at school together. Lorca was five years older than Dali and destined to become one of the great poets of the twentieth

DALI AND LORCA

Dali studied at the Royal Academy of San Fernando from 1921 to 1923, where he was introduced to a whole new world of innovative artists, freethinkers, radical politicos, and intellectuals. He made many friends, and best among them was Federico Garcia Lorca. Even today, the exact nature of the relationship between these extremely close young artists remains a mystery.

Lorca was six years older than Dali and a homosexual. Dali, on the other hand, was an inexperienced young man, who was somewhat immature in his understanding of male sexuality. As close as the two men were, did they become sexual lovers? This question leads to the greater question about Dali's own personal sexual preferences, not just while in art school, but during his entire life. The answers are complicated.

That Lorca and Dali shared intellectual ideas is evident. The two, together with other artist friends living at the "Resi," developed their own artistic language, slang, and terminology. Much of their artistic theory was based on ideas unique to them and not easily understood by others. They often spoke in a personal, artistic code. Dali and others in the group rejected much of the old style and subject matter of earlier art. They railed against the romantic elements they saw in such works. These earlier subjects had been painted to appeal to middle-class European tastes. Their dislike for these bourgeois values became embodied in a term the group coined—*putrefacto*. Dali drew pictures of the despised "putrefactos," depicting these middle-class Spaniards with an art-driven loathing, and Lorca wrote unflattering poems directed against them. The two men shared many such values and theories about the arts.

Was there a physical relationship the two men shared, as

century. He was also a playwright whose noted works includes *Yerma, The House of Bernarda Alba,* and *Blood Wedding.* Unfortunately, in 1936, during the Spanish Civil War, he was

well? Federico Garcia Lorca was, indeed, a dark and handsome man, one whom Dali and others found charming. As the two men deepened their relationship over time, Dali became some- what obsessive about Lorca, desiring to paint him several times. Dali did invite Lorca to spend the summer of 1925 with him at his family's seaside home at Cadaques. Lorca did, it seems, fall in love with Dali and wanted a relationship. He even wrote a poem about Dali, titled "Ode to Salvador Dali," which included the lines:

> O Salvador Dali, with an olive-smooth voice,
> I'll speak of what your person and pictures speak to me.
> No praise for your imperfect adolescent brush,
> But rather sing of the perfect path of your arrows.*

In another line, the poet writes: "May stars like falconless fists shine on you, while your painting and your life break into flower."**

Did Dali respond to Lorca's advances? Perhaps. In his adult writings, however, Dali claims he and Lorca did not have a rela- tionship. Though Dali probably struggled with such tendencies (in his later years, Dali became an outspoken admirer of young men who had significant female tendencies), he was probably not a homosexual. At the same time, though, he had a lifelong dread of heterosexual relations.

* Robert Goff, *The Essential Salvador Dali* (New York: Harry N. Abrams, 1998), 36.
** Robert Anderson, *Salvador Dali* (Danbury, Conn.: Franklin Watts, 2002), 12.

violently executed by a firing squad under the command of General Francisco Franco, the leader of the right-wing Fascists.

Although throughout his life Dali enjoyed his personal time and solitude, he was outgoing with his comrades at the Academy. He took up his quarters at La Residencia de Estudiantes, the "Resi," where he came in contact with other artists in training, as well as a circle of writers and intellectuals. (The "Resi" was an offshoot of the Institución Libre de Enseñanza, "The Free Teaching Institution," which was a progressive secondary school.) The school was "free" in that it educated separately from control by the Catholic Church or the government. The "Resi" could accommodate 150 students, many of whom lived there because of their independent mindedness and spirit of free thinking. He, Lorca, Buñuel, and others became known for their wild lifestyle, as they frequented the night scene and café world of Madrid. Dali pursued his penchant for strange, erratic behavior, regularly displaying it in public. He became known for placing a banknote in his drink, allowing it to dissolve, then downing it.

The Royal Academy of San Fernando was awash in opportunities for intellectual and artistic stimulation. Guest speakers came to deliver addresses and important ideas at the Residencia; these included scientists Madame Curie and Albert Einstein; popular science fiction writer H.G. Wells; economist John Maynard Keynes; and a host of others. Through his studies, Dali became more acquainted with other contemporary painters—a school of French surrealists that included Louis Aragon, Jacques Baron, André Breton, and Paul Éluard, as well as a school of cubist artists that included Picasso, Georges Braque, and Juan Gris. The young art student spent countless hours wandering through the galleries of Spain's greatest museum, the Prado. Through exposure to both the works of Europe's grand masters of art, as well as contemporary artists, Dali formed his personal attitudes, opinions, and appreciations about art and its painters. (It did not take him long to become disappointed in his instructors at the Academy.)

Although his early paintings had been influenced by the French impressionists, pointillists, the fauvists, and the paintings of Pierre Bonnard, he soon rejected them. Now he was adopting and adapting the approach of the cubists.

AN EXPERIMENT WITH CUBISM

Cubism originated as an avant-garde artistic movement around 1909. Its originators included the famous Spanish artist Pablo Picasso and the Frenchman Georges Braque. The goal of cubism was to put aside an artistic style by which subjects were painted to depict them in the traditional three-dimensional perspective. Instead, cubist artists sought to present their subjects with "overlapping and rearranged fragments that evoked the subject's inherent complexity."[43]

Dali became fascinated with the cubist paintings of two fellow Spanish painters, Picasso and Juan Gris. In 1923, he painted a work that he titled *Self-Portrait with "La Publicitat,"* which bears the direct stamp of inspiration from both Picasso and Braque. Although such works usually resulted in the complete fragmentation of every recognizable form in the painting, Dali is careful not to dissect his own face in this work. It is the only portion of the painting not cut into multiple fragments, the "cubes" of cubism. To some art historians, it is Dali's way of saying "that cubism, no matter how important, can never disassemble the great Dali."[44] He painted other cubism-inspired works, such as his *Still Life: Sandia*, which he created in 1924. The work features a bowl of fruit as part of a table setting that also includes a drinking glass, napkins, and a tablecloth. Although the elements of the painting are clear and recognizable (which is not always the case in extreme examples of cubism), the painting, again, is the direct result of inspiration from similar works by other cubists, especially the older Picasso. Another of Dali's cubist works was also directly impacted by Picasso, at least in its subject matter. Dali's *Pierrot Playing the Guitar* (1925) included such Picasso elements as the guitar and the Pierrot, a clownish character popular in

French pantomimes. Both were used by Picasso in his cubist compositions. Dali took cubism down a different path, however; he reworked the artistic style as his own, which included fantasy and a metaphysical viewpoint. Symbols lie scattered at the feet of the hatted, pipe-smoking Pierrot (who really has no feet at all, his legs resembling something closer to elongated saw blades), including a wine bottle, glass, flute, and playing cards—one of which is the ace of hearts. Outside the Pierrot's starkly cast room, a small sailboat passes calmly by, floating on a smooth blue sea, followed by a pair of thin companion clouds. It is Dali toying with Picasso.

There is also a psychological aspect to the painting. Behind the Pierrot stands a dark, shrouded figure, as though it were his shadow. It is likely that Dali intended his friend Lorca to represent the Pierrot and the shadow as himself. The painting embodies Dali's feelings that he and Lorca became such close friends that they became one and the same person.

BEYOND CUBISM

As Dali continued to experiment with his art, he tried various styles beyond cubism, and other art styles gained his interest and attention. In the years following World War I (1914–1918), the art world began to experience other changes and redirections. Many of the experimental art forms— including cubism, fauvism, expressionism, and even impressionism—no longer interested this new, restless generation of painters. These artists began to return to realism as the basic foundation of their art. Yet their new form of "realism" would be innovative, even disturbing, to the art-consuming public. One such painter of this new realism, which would become known as surrealism, was the Italian artist Giorgio de Chirico. De Chirico turned his back on the bold, wildly exciting canvases of the fauvists, such as Matisse, and completely rejected the fragmented, self-conscious canvases of Picasso and cubism. Instead, he painted using muted, even somber colors and returned to a traditional three-dimensional perspective.

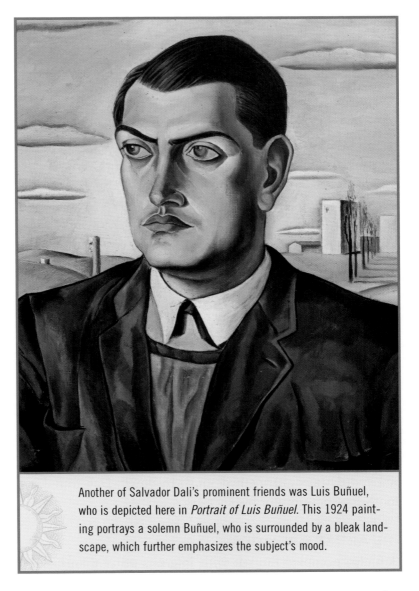

Another of Salvador Dali's prominent friends was Luis Buñuel, who is depicted here in *Portrait of Luis Buñuel*. This 1924 painting portrays a solemn Buñuel, who is surrounded by a bleak landscape, which further emphasizes the subject's mood.

His art was not without innovation, however. He recast his new realism by creating eerie, ethereal images, placing his human figures in the midst of overshadowing, impersonal landscapes and urbanscapes, where the overriding themes were centered in darkness and shadowy worlds. The purpose of such stylistic canvases was to create a fantastic vision using unrelated imagery in an effort to portray the subconscious mind.

Whether the elements of the painting were logical or comprehensible made no difference to the painter.

As for Dali, he took to this artistic style with great excitement. He used his 1924 *Portrait of Luis Buñuel* to place his sober-faced, black-suited friend in the foreground against a backdrop of a lifeless, abandoned landscape. Gloom spreads across Buñuel's face and across the barren hills behind the painting's solitary subject.

Even though Dali had close friends at the Royal Academy of San Fernando and enjoyed their comradeship, he also spent time alone, working on his art. Many of his days were filled with "a quiet existence, secluding himself in his small dorm room and painting around the clock."[45] During his year in residence, his quarters filled up with canvases, making it difficult for visitors to maneuver around his artistic collection. The arts consumed him completely. He further developed his talents, and his drawing skills greatly impressed his art teachers. His disappointment with the restrictions in the Academy curriculum led him to paint subjects and in styles of his choosing. He continually paid weekend visits to the Prado, the great repository of Western art. He developed an admiration for the works of Renaissance painter Hieronymus Bosch (1450–1516), whose allegorical landscapes pictured metaphysical worlds, including hell and damned, tormented souls. In Bosch, Dali found yet another inspiration for his later art.

THE ARTIST'S POLITICS

Dali also occupied himself with interests other than his art. Politics was beginning to play a more significant role in the life of the young Salvador, as he approached his 20s. While he was still a teenager, a revolution erupted in Czarist Russia that resulted in the establishment of a Communist government led by V.I. Lenin. Dali was keenly interested in radical politics and became a supporter of the Russian Revolution. (Although he never became a supporter of Communism itself.) Through these years of his late teens and early 20s, Salvador became an anarchist. He supported independence for his homeland, Catalonia, from Spain. Then, in September 1923, General Miguel Primo de Rivera came to power and established military rule in Spain. For the next seven years, Spain was governed by a moderate military dictatorship. The elder Dali opposed the military regime. Partly because of his father's outspoken criticism of the government and because of his radical political views, Dali was arrested, along with two of his friends, in May 1924, and jailed. (At the time, King Alfonso XIII was scheduled to visit Catalonia, and the government took the precaution of arresting any possible troublemakers.) Dali spent just over a month in jail and did not seem to mind the experience much. He spent his time drawing. On June 11, he was ordered to be released by a military judge after no charges were filed.

Dali also ran afoul of Academy officials in 1923, when he engaged in a student protest against the hiring of an art instructor, Daniel Vázquez Diaz, whom students felt was unqualified for the position. Dali left the Academy from 1923 to 1924, but he continued to paint and attended drawing classes at the Free Academy in Madrid. In time, he moved back to Figueres, where he again studied under his former art teacher Juan Núñez and spent time making some of his first etchings and artistic prints.

A NEW INFLUENCE

That same year—1923—Dali was introduced to the writings of the father of psychology, Sigmund Freud. Freud's famous study, *The Interpretation of Dreams*, which had first been published before Dali was born, was reissued that year in a Spanish edition. (Dali's personal copy of the book, with his handwritten marginal notes, still exists in a private collection.) When Dali read the work, his life changed dramatically:

> Dali found a liberating conceptual framework just at the time when the Surrealist movement was developing in Paris. When

one realizes that psychological theory came to Dali when he was at his most susceptible, it is easy to appreciate why he clutched it so fervently. He immersed himself in it and forever after thought of Freud as the one person to whom he was most indebted—a debt he personally expressed to Freud when he met him in London in 1938. There is little doubt that Freudian concepts—such as free association, dream narration, dream symbolism, condensation, displacement, and sublimation—found fruitful parallels in Dali's paintings.[46]

Dali used his understanding of Freudian theories to explain himself, his paranoia, his hang-ups, even his excessive behavior. The subconscious, personal memory, imagination, and fantasy—all important subjects to Freud—became part of Dali's artistic form of expression.

Surrealism

AN INTRODUCTION TO PARIS

By the fall of 1925, Dali, now a young man of 21, returned to the Royal Academy of San Fernando and resumed his classes. His art was already receiving notice, and, in November, he had his first solo exhibition at Barcelona's prestigious Galería Dalmau. His impressionist, cubist, and fauvist works received good reviews from critics. Picasso himself attended Dali's show and was impressed by what he saw. Among the works on display in the show was a neo-cubist painting, *Venus and the Sailor* (1925), which was reminiscent of Picasso's earlier, realistic style. (Neo-cubism was a type of cubism in which the subjects are created using simplified planes and shapes that do not abandon the larger elements of reality.) Other works included his *Portrait of My Father* and *Girl Standing at the Window*, both of which were painted in 1925. (The girl in the painting was his sister, Ana Maria.)

Of the three, the one most unique to a truly Dali-inspired style

In 1925, Salvador Dali had his first solo exhibition, which was held at Barcelona's prestigious Galería Dalmau. Among the paintings displayed was *Venus and the Sailor*, a neo-cubist oil painting reminiscent of Pablo Picasso's earlier works.

was the portrait of Ana Maria. The painting features a neatly dressed woman, her back to the viewer, staring out a lightly draped window toward a seascape; a sailboat barely perceptible along the distant shore moves along the Figueres harbor. The painting is a portrait of loneliness, detachment, and longing. The viewer not only enters the sparse room but takes in the view seen by the woman. There is no connection made with the woman's face, but her feelings transcend the canvas. The viewer feels what she feels. To create this work, Dali abandoned his impressionist techniques, as well as his cubist experiments, and painted his subjects with an extreme level of realism, which can be seen in his works from this point forward.

The next spring, Dali took his first visit to Paris, the great European art center. An aunt and his sister, Ana Maria, accompanied him. There he met Buñuel, who introduced him to the leading modern artists in the City of Light, including Picasso. The visit to Paris inspired Dali, who came to understand that his creative destiny lay in Paris. While there, he visited all the important attractions that appealed to a young, modern artist, including various cafés, the Grevin Museum, the Louvre, the palace grounds at Versailles, and the studio of nineteenth-century French realist Jean-François Millet, whose work Dali admired. In the Louvre, Salvador and Ana Maria spent hours wandering the galleries. Dali was "literally in ecstasy"[47] viewing the works of Leonardo da Vinci, Raphael, and the French painter Ingres.

By the summer of 1926, Dali had returned to Figueres and was preparing to take his graduation exams at the Royal Academy of San Fernando. Tired and disappointed in art school, though, Dali refused to take the exams, because he believed that the faculty was not talented enough to judge his work. He was subsequently expelled and over the next year, his art took him in a number of different directions. He was still experimenting and still under the influence of Picasso, as evidenced by his neo-cubist painting *Figure on the Rocks*. That fall, he prepared for his second solo exhibition, again in Barcelona. The show was held from December 1926 through January 1927 and was also a critical success.

A MYSTERIOUS LANDSCAPE

Over the next nine months, Dali carried out his compulsory military service (required of all young Spanish men) and was able to produce no paintings. When he did return to his art, his style had changed dramatically. He had turned himself over, not only to realism but to the surrealists. Before he did so, though, he painted an exquisitely realist work that he titled *The Basket of Bread* (1926). The work shows the impact the Old Masters and their extreme reliance on realistic subject portrayal had on Dali at the time. Technically, the work is a sublime masterpiece in its simplicity and in the painter's skill it represents. The subject is the title, nothing more than a woven basket of sliced and broken bread, set upon a table linen against an unlit, black background. The scene has a natural setting, one that is entirely domestic. The soft light and shadows give the bread and its simple container an almost religious quality, however, causing them to take on the symbolism of an answered prayer: "Give us this day, our daily bread." To accomplish such a purely realistic and technically satisfying painting, Dali was working under the influence of the paintings he had studied for years, including those of the great Dutch painter Jan Vermeer and fellow Spaniards Velázquez and Zurbarán. Another canvas followed, again somewhat realistic, but, again, impacted by Picasso. His *Femme Couchee* ("Reclining Woman") is another neo-cubist work. The subject is less the woman and more about a study of "the geometry of the oversize, supine figure, suggestive of a starfish on a beach."[48]

Even as Dali created these canvases of absolute and cubist-based realism, though, he would soon paint an explosive, eerie landscape inhabited by a collection of seemingly unrelated elements, including a mysterious cone-and-obelisk-symbol dominating the central portion of the canvas, which resulted in a fantasy painting of early Daliesque dimensions. His *Apparatus and Hand* was painted in 1927.

Commanding the center and focal point of Dali's *Apparatus and Hand* is a strange pair of geometric shapes, perhaps a leftover from his cubist experiments, surrounded by smaller but entirely symbolic elements delivered to the canvas as if from a dream. Although Picasso obviously influenced Dali's work, another source of inspiration is present here, too—the Viennese psychoanalyst Sigmund Freud.

These two shapes, a cone and an inverted obelisk, defy the laws of physics, as the point of the obelisk balances itself on the base of the cone, whereas the cone stands on spindly stilts. These are the "apparatus" portion of the painting—objects that exist in a timeless, spaceless world, where the normal restraints, laws, and tensions of the real world—the conscious world—no longer apply.

Additional symbols occupy Dali's dreamlike landscape. The cubist-inspired cardboard cutout of a woman stands to the right of the apparatus, and a plaster cast of a woman's torso floats in space, alongside a flayed fish and a nearly translucent donkey. Some symbols indicated Dali's sexual hang-ups, others his loathing of those who refuse to defy convention, as seen in the donkey. The donkey, as in other Dali works, represents the putrefaction, "the rotting conventional thought of the bourgeoisie."[49]

It is clear with this work that surrealism was taking over Dali's creativity. With it, he abandons the cubist elements and the geometric studies found in *Femme Couchee*. Space in the painting is not limited to reality any longer, any more than subject matter is bound by realism. Thus, this work depicts an unearthly world in which objects float in space, strange objects dominate, and Dali's mind opens up to limitless visions. To the average viewer, the world depicted makes no sense, but that is the nature of surrealism.

DALI AND THE MOVEMENT

Dali was introduced to surrealism not only as a painter, but in other fields as well, including film. Early in 1929, Dali made a second trip to Paris, and he convinced his father to pay for it. There, he met up with his old friend Luis Buñuel, who had

In 1929, Salvador Dali and his friend Luis Buñuel (pictured here) collaborated on a 17-minute film titled *Un Chien Andalou*, "An Andalusian Dog." Described as the first surrealist movie, the film served to shock and confuse its audience with disturbing images.

already moved permanently to Paris. Together, they began collaborating on a surrealist film they would title *Un Chien Andalou*, "An Andalusian Dog." It would become a groundbreaking piece of film art for the surrealist movement. The film would be financed by Buñuel's mother.

From the beginning, Dali and Buñuel had wanted to create a film like no other ever made. As Buñuel explained to a friend, "The aim is to produce something absolutely new in the history of the cinema. We hope to make visible certain subconscious states which we believe can only be expressed by the cinema."[50] The pairing of the creative minds of Dali and Buñuel seemed perfectly matched for the experimental project. Writing a half century later, Buñuel described how well he and Dali worked together:

> We were so attuned to each other that there was no argument. We wrote accepting the first images that occurred to us, systematically rejecting those deriving from culture or education. They had to be images which surprised us, and which we both accepted without discussion. Only that.[51]

The result of this close, artistic cooperation was a 17-minute film that included images designed to confuse and shock its audience. In one scene, ants crawl out of a hole in a man's hand. In another, a dead donkey lies atop a grand piano. The most shocking is a razor slicing across a girl's eye (Dali and Buñuel actually shot the close-up scene by using an ox eye.) When completed, the disturbing film played in art houses in Paris and other cities and was considered a great success by the surrealists. Breton himself declared it "the first surrealist film."[52] The film managed to bring Dali into the circle of the Parisian surrealists.

GALA ENTERS HIS LIFE

As Dali became more attracted to surrealism, his personal and professional life took several new turns. His friendship with Lorca began to cool, as Dali became less enchanted with his intellectual comrade. Lorca was not putting the kind of subject matter into his poetry that Dali expected of him, including lines about "20th century inventions like automobiles, planes, and American jazz."[53] As Dali turned away from his relationship with Lorca, he was beginning a new friendship, this time with a woman—Gala Éluard. Dali first met Gala in the summer of 1929, during a visit she and her husband made to Cadaques. Her husband, Paul Éluard, was a famous surrealist

(continued on page 59)

LUIS BUÑUEL AND THE SURREALISTS

When Salvador Dali arrived at the Royal Academy of San Fernando to begin his serious art studies, he came into contact with other students who would have a significant impact on his work as he developed his talents and direction as an artist. This group included Federico Garcia Lorca, José Bello, Pedro Garfias, and the young man destined to have a major impact on Dali's interest in the cinema, Luis Buñuel. Several of these fellow students would become significant figures in the developing school of art, literature, and cinema known as surrealism. During the 1920s, Dali came into contact with other leading surrealists, including André Breton, who was the self-proclaimed messiah of the movement.

Lorca and Buñuel probably had the greatest impact on Dali as an artist. Dali and Lorca became extremely close friends and confidants, as well as fellow surrealists—although Lorca's work was centered in literature and poetry, rather than art. As for Buñuel, the pioneering surrealist filmmaker would have a profound effect on Salvador Dali's artistic eye.

Luis Buñuel and Salvador Dali were alike in important ways. Both were the eldest of five children and had dominated their parents' attentions. According to one historian, young Buñuel "enjoyed the unconditional indulgence of his young, adoring and beautiful mother."* While Dali always fretted about his appearance, Buñuel was decidedly obsessed with his. He was "a manic keep-fit fiend."** His daily workout regime included running, jumping, boxing, and calisthenics. He was always "lying down and asking people to jump on his tummy."***

Together, Buñuel and Dali produced one of the first surrealist films, *Un Chien Andalou*, "An Andalusian Dog" (1929). The purpose of the film was to create something completely new for European screen audiences. Among the film's visuals was a scene in which a woman's eye is sliced with a razorblade (an ox eye was actually used in filming). Their second film was titled *L'Age d'Or*, "The Golden Age" (1930), which includes a controversial portrayal of Jesus that was adapted from the work of eighteenth-century French writer Marquis de Sade. Dali, in fact, quit work on the film before its completion after the two artists disagreed on its anti-Catholic content.

Although Dali did not continue to collaborate on future films with Buñuel, his surrealist companion continued to make controversial films. In 1932, Buñuel produced another film, *Land without Bread*, which presented the Catholic Church in an extremely negative light (Buñuel's anti-Catholic tendencies never completely sat well with Dali.) As Buñuel became more recognized as a filmmaker, his work was picked up by major studios. By the 1930s, Buñuel was doing dubbing work for Paramount in Paris and working on projects for Warner Brothers in Spain. By the late 1930s, Buñuel left Spain during the Spanish Civil War, immigrating to the United States. He did archival work with the Museum of Modern Art in New York and then moved to Hollywood, where he produced film remakes in Spanish; work that preceded the studios' technique of re-dubbing dialogue in other languages.

Following World War II, Buñuel landed in Mexico and soon set out on an exciting leg of his film career. Working with producer Oscar Dancigers, Buñuel made a series of films in Spanish that brought him further international acclaim. In these films, including *Los Olvidados* (1950) and *Criminal Life of Archibaldo de la Cruz* (1955), Buñuel developed his combined approach of surrealist humor and social commentary. He gave special attention to the plight of the average Mexican. Through these films, he became the most famous director of Spanish-speaking films.

With the passing of the golden age of Mexican filmmaking, Buñuel returned to Europe by the late 1950s and continued to make films through the late 1970s. He retired to Mexico and died there in 1983.

Throughout the decades, Buñuel never abandoned his surrealist ideas—he remained devoted to including disturbing images in his films. After he retired, he wrote an autobiography in which he made a wholly surrealist statement that he would be pleased if all the copies of his films were destroyed. In that same work, he referred to his early days with Salvador Dali, in which he made the claim that it was he who had "discovered" Dali and helped make him famous.

Although Dali and Buñuel did not remain close throughout their lives (they had a serious falling out in 1939, when Dali refused to loan money to Buñuel), they did keep up sporadic contact. In 1983, toward the end of Buñuel's life, he received a telegram from Dali, suggesting they collaborate on another film. Buñuel appeared to appreciate the offer from his famous friend but declined, telegramming Dali back: GREAT IDEA FOR FILM LITTLE DEMON BUT I WITHDREW FROM THE CINEMA FIVE YEARS AGO AND NEVER GO OUT NOW. A PITY.

To the end, Buñuel remained unwavering in his support of surrealism and other convictions. One of the driving forces for Buñuel was his anti-Catholic sentiments, which were the result of his own concept of social justice and his lifelong affinity for atheism. Toward the end of his life, in an interview, he was asked if he was still an atheist. His answer was both ironic and surreal: "Thank god, I'm still an atheist."†

* Ian Gibson, *The Shameful Life of Salvador Dali* (New York: W.W. Norton & Company, 1997), 133.
** Ibid.
*** Ibid.
† *http://en.wikipedia.org/wiki/Luis_Bu%C3%B1uel*

(*continued from page 55*)
poet. In the company of the Éluards were the artist Rene Magritte and his wife, Georgette, as well as Dali's old friend Buñuel and an important art dealer, Camille Goemans. (Goemans had introduced Dali to Paul Éluard early in the summer, in Paris, at a fashionable night club.)

Salvador Dali's introduction to Gala Éluard would change his life forever. He had heard of her from friends, as well as from her husband, Paul, long before he met her. He had begun to fantasize about her, perhaps after seeing photos shown to him by her husband. When he met her for the first time, she was attired in a bathing suit on the beach at Es Llane. He instantly fell in love. As for Gala, she was not immediately attracted to Dali; in fact, she may have initially found him repulsive. In time, though, she would become intrigued by him and by his behavior:

> His manic and intense personality alarmed her, yet she sensed a boyish helplessness beneath the surface. One day she took Dali by the hand and silenced his fanatical laughter for a moment. Dali saw a way out of the abyss and fell at her feet. Gala became his muse and the object of his intense passion; she later became his wife and companion for life.[54]

It may be that Gala arrived in Dali's life at just the right time. He had begun to act exceedingly erratic and was prone to manic activity, as well as depression. His painting was becoming obsessive to him and everything revolved around the surreal. Psychologically, he "became pray to delirious fantasies and suffered a full hallucination. Bouts of hysterical laughter gripped him, rendering him incapable of speech or movement."[55] Gala took control of Dali, and the two were rarely separated for any length of time for the rest of their lives. They would remain partners for more than a half century and Gala would become his business manager. Dali became so attached and dependent on Gala that, by 1931, he included her name in his signature—Dali-Gala.

Who was this woman who could exert such control over Salvador Dali? Gala was born Helena Diakonoff Deluvina in Russia in 1894. She had taken the name Gala while still quite young. One of four siblings, her father was a prosperous Jewish lawyer. She and Paul Éluard had married in 1917, but they had had an open marriage, and sometimes shared their bed with a third person. Gala was known as "charmingly seductive and mercilessly cold."[56] The year Dali and Gala met, she was 35 years old and he was 10 years younger. Just as Dali had heard of her before their meeting, she had been told of Dali by her husband, Paul. "Eluard kept telling me about his handsome Dali," she explained later. "I felt he was almost pushing me into his arms before I even saw him."[57] Buñuel saw the attraction between the two immediately: "Overnight Dali changed beyond recognition."[58] Before the end of summer, Paul Éluard left for Paris, but Gala stayed behind in Cadaques with Dali. The two continued developing what would become a unique, lifelong relationship.

Dali became infatuated with Gala, but his father was not pleased. Don Salvador Dali Cusi disapproved of his son taking up with a French woman, especially one who "was married as well as sexy and shameless."[59] Dali did not break off their relationship, though, and by September 1929, the elder Salvador cut him out of his will. His estate was bequeathed to Ana Maria. That step by his father was only the beginning, however. By December 6, Salvador Dali received a letter from his infuriated and disappointed father, informing him of his "irrevocable banishment"[60] from the family home. The younger Dali responded immediately by shaving off his hair and burying it in the sandy beach at Es Llane. Emotionally, Dali's response is more veiled. Perhaps he saw this move on the part of his father as liberating him, making a permanent move to Paris possible. A week later, Salvador left Cadaques, taking a taxi to the train station, where an express train was scheduled to leave for Paris. Dali later wrote about his departure from Cadaques and his family:

The road that goes from Cadaques . . . makes a series of twists and turns, from each of which the village . . . can be seen receding farther into the distance. One of these turns is the last from which one can still see Cadaques, which has become a tiny speck . . . Never had I neglected to turn around for this last glance at Cadaques. But on this day, when the taxi came to the bend in the road, instead of turning my head I continued to look straight before me.[61]

Dali did not see his father again until 1948, nearly 20 years later.

Despite the relationship they began in the summer of 1929, Dali and Gala parted, at least for the moment. When Gala finally left to return to her husband at summer's end, Dali had given her the painting he had been working on when she, Paul, and their entourage arrived earlier in the season—*The Lugubrious Game* (which is also known as *Dismal Sport*). The painting had confused but fascinated Paul Éluard, and he had left Gala with instructions to procure it from Dali for their personal collection, which she did. The painting serves as another early example of Dali's increasing tendencies toward surrealism. The picture contains more floating images and strange manifestations of both human and fantasy subjects. Everything is symbolic, a manifestation of dreams and paranoiac visions: A grasshopper represents Dali's fears; lions symbolize animal aggression; Dali's sleeping head and a woman's hand denote a repressed sexuality; and the bearded man in the foreground is Dali's disapproving father figure.

The Golden Age

ACCEPTED INTO THE CIRCLE

Cut off from his father and banished from his home, Dali left Cadaques and headed for Paris and Gala. In the months that followed, the younger Dali had his more recent works—*The Lugubrious Game, The Sacred Heart, The Accommodation of Desire*, and others, including his *Portrait of Paul Eluard*—shown at an exhibition at Camille Goemans' gallery in Paris. The Goemans show lasted from November 20 to December 5. The show did not make Dali the new sensation of the Parisian art world and over the next few years, Salvador would struggle with his art and its acceptance.

During those years, however, he did not abandon his love of surrealism. He even became more committed to the validity of the art style. Once in Paris, he entered the surrealist circle, and Breton accepted him as a new member whose talent was extensive, raw, and original. Gala was at his side, having abandoned Paul Éluard. Dali

Among the leading surrealists of the 1920s and 1930s were Paul Éluard, André Breton, and Robert Desnos, pictured here left to right. Breton's *Manifesto of Surrealism* was published in 1924 and served to define surrealism as a way of thinking without reason, logic, or other mental guidelines, including moral or aesthetic concerns.

was developing his own special approach to art, his paranoiac-critical philosophy. It was a philosophy he wrote about the following year, in 1930, in a work he also illustrated, titled *La Femme Visible*, "The Visible Woman." (He dedicated the art manifesto to Gala.) Dali's paranoiac-critical ideas would remain important to him throughout his life, and he was indebted to the surrealists' concept of "pure psychic automatism," which Breton had espoused in his own writings, including his *Manifesto of Surrealism*, which dated from the origins of the movement in 1924. Breton defined his psychic automatism as a "pure state, by which one proposes to express . . . the actual functioning of thought."[62] He was referring to thought without reason, logic, or other mental guidelines, including moral or aesthetic concerns. According to Breton, automatism called for a conscious collapse into one's own self, into the human consciousness and the "world of the unknown within."[63] In the end, for Dali, his paranoiac-critical approach to his art placed his subject matter on a Freudian level, and his pictures often contained symbolism, often sexual, as well as what appears to be completely unrelated subject matter, placed side by side on the canvas.

To the untrained, uninformed observer, then, Dali's paintings often appear nonsensical and unfocused, as his landscapes are filled with unearthly shapes and beings, and the laws of physics seem to have taken a vacation. Objects float, they fly, concrete realities fade and, sometimes, even melt. All this was Dali's way of projecting the deepest recesses of his mind to his art. As his various mental images appear, serving as what he called "guideposts to the mind,"[64] he opened the cluttered closet of his subconscious. He draws on his dreams as he draws his art. In doing so, he developed paintings based on "a spontaneous method of irrational associations."[65] As Breton himself explained, an artist or writer would create something "as beautiful as the chance encounter between a sewing machine and an umbrella upon a dissecting table."[66] The trip of moving items from one's subconscious to the canvas could be tricky, though. There were times when Dali himself seemed on the verge of total madness, but he was aware of crossing this thin line. In his words: "The only difference between myself and a madman is that I am not mad."[67]

EXPLORING THE SUBCONSCIOUS

The early 1930s, then, was a time of creative output framed by economic struggle for Salvador Dali. He produced such surrealist-driven paintings as *The Average Bureaucrat, Shades of Night Descending, Au Bord de la Mer,* and *Memory of the Child-Woman,* all of which were psychological works painted between 1931 and 1932. Each of these works was based on the painter's difficult personal life and his exploration of his dream-based subconscious world. Only surrealism could serve as the platform to make these paintings acceptable or even possible. Dali was tackling Freud, and each painting, with its complicated symbols, is a metaphor for something otherwise existing only in "Dali's own complex, emotionally ambivalent state at the time."[68] Both Gala and Dali's father serve as motivators for the paintings. Dali's relationship with his father was especially tense and estranged while Gala was ill (she ultimately had to have a hysterectomy), which probably jarred Dali's sense of anxious dread. One other figure probably also helped determine the content of these surrealist paintings. Salvador took lessons in shadowing from the Italian surrealist Giorgio de Chirico and the rocks of Cadeques' Cape Reus play an important role in each work.

Dali's paintings were not selling, however. Life in Paris became difficult, both economically and professionally. It was an expensive place to live. He was becoming famous but was on the verge of creative insanity. In 1930, he collaborated on a second film with Buñuel, this one titled *L'Age d'Or*, "The Golden Age." As with their first film, this work was a haunting montage of "archbishops and bones among the rocks of Cape Reus, a blind man being ill-treated, a dog crushed to death, a son killed by his father, and a character from [the Marquis] de Sade disguised as Christ."[69] The film was filled with violence and revolting scenes. Showings of the film caused violence of its own, including an incident in a Parisian theatre, where pro-Hitler youth, the Camelots du Roy, rose up in moral indignation and destroyed the cinema house. Shortly thereafter, Parisian police banned the film.

Not only was Paris an expensive place to live, but it was also home to many distractions that kept Dali from his work. He grew homesick for Spain, for Cadaques and Figueres. Gala kept him in the art capital of Paris, though, and put pressure on friends of hers who were art dealers to support Dali's work.

After a few years, Gala's insistence that they remain in Paris paid off. *L'Age d'Or* had been financed by a French aristocrat, the Viscount Charles de Noailles, and his wife, the Viscountess Marie-Laurie de Noailles. The couple had recently purchased Dali's painting *Dismal Sport*. (The Éluards had given the painting to Goemans to sell after Gala returned with it to Paris during the summer of 1929.) The Noailles would soon become Dali's first important benefactors.

The Noailles—two of France's most important patrons of art and literature—had previously been introduced to Buñuel. They were great admirers of Dali and Buñuel's first film, *Un Chien Andalou*, which Charles had paid to screen at his estate in the family's personal theater in July 1929. Buñuel was invited to the showing at the Noailles'. At first, the surrealist filmmaker was skeptical of the Noailles, uncertain they really understood the nature of his film or of the surrealists' goals in general, but he was soon convinced. Later in life, he confessed of the Noailles: "I've never met art patrons as generous as them. They had exemplary discretion, grace, good taste and consideration."[70] Thanks to the Noailles, others began viewing the film, and Charles and Marie-Laurie made certain Buñuel and Dali were paid for each viewing.

A NEWFOUND AUDIENCE

Dali's film was gaining an audience, and as a result, his reputation began to grow within the surrealist circle in Paris. In 1930, he was selected to design the title image of a new statement published by the surrealists, *The Second Surrealist Manifesto*. That year, Dali also published his own vision of surrealism— *The Visible Woman*. In this important personal manifesto, Dali expressed the hope that surrealists would produce their art while feverishly driven by commitment. He believed the ultimate artistic achievement was one that depicted one view of its subject at one moment and another view of the same subject as well. The only difference would be determined by the fallible vision of the viewer's psyche. In one respect, Dali meant to depict two views of the same subject, based on optical illusion. An image first appears as a wine goblet, only to be next seen as a human face, whose shape is determined by the goblet. It was a form of dual depiction he would engage in frequently.

As Dali's work gained prestige among the leading surrealists in Paris, the Noailles invited Dali and Gala to their mansion at 11 Place des Etats Unis, in Paris. Already, they owned one of the most important Parisian collections of modern and avant-garde art, and they were interested in Dali's work. The Noailleses could not have come into Dali's life at a better time for the Spanish artist. The art dealer Camille Goemans would go bankrupt in 1931, forcing him to close his gallery (his wife had run off with another man) and leaving Dali with nearly no support. Charles Noailles soon came to Salvador's rescue, however. Not only did Noailles agree to finance Dali and Buñuel's second film, but he was going to buy additional paintings from him. That year—1931—Dali sold another painting, *The Old Age of William Tell*, to the French aristocratic couple. Charles also lined up another art dealer, Pierre Colle, for Dali.

The Noailles helped Dali in another extraordinary way, as well. According to Dali, he first asked Charles to purchase a run-down boat shack so he could set up a studio in the small village of Port Lligat, just down the road from the town of Cadaques. Charles agreed, advancing Dali 20,000 francs, just as Dali had requested. Dali had the shack fixed up, and it became an important place for the development of Dali's art and his relationship with Gala. (When Dali's father learned his son and Gala were moving back to Cadaques, he went into a rage, but there was little he could do to stop them.)

Dali had returned to his home again; for Cadaques, its beaches, and its mysterious coastal rock shapes represented "the spot he repeatedly said he loved best in the world."[71] This house would be their home for the rest of their lives. Over the years, as Dali's wealth increased, the couple would add on to the small fisherman's cottage. (Today, the once tiny house is a rambling hodgepodge of rooms that serve as a museum

This lithograph of Salvador Dali's most famous painting, *The Persistence of Memory*, is pictured here at an exhibit in Fort Worth, Texas, in 2004. Dali came up with the melting watch theme after eating some Camembert cheese, which had turned soft and gooey, much like the watches in his painting.

dedicated to Dali's art.) It was also in the house at Port Lligat that Dali produced one of the most famous paintings of his art career—*The Persistence of Memory*.

THE PERSISTENCE OF MEMORY

Dali's painting of *The Persistence of Memory* reveals a stylized maturity on the part of the surrealist painter. The work is well balanced and composed, and its subject is subtly chosen, more so than in his earlier surrealist works, which come off so crowded, so kinetic, so difficult to focus on clearly—each bearing multiple messages through endless symbols. With this painting, the images are limited; there is a depth and balance that became a recurring theme for the artist throughout his later works.

The work is a masterpiece of "carefully chosen unconscious material that crystallizes Dali's paranoiac-critical method."[72] At the center and foreground of the painting are three enigmatic, melting timepieces that symbolize how unreliable the real world of solid objects and the conscious world of the nondreaming can really be. The watches droop over items that include a leafless and lifeless olive tree, a square block of stone, and a resting amoeba-shaped head to symbolize the artist himself. (To watchful viewers, it is the same head found in earlier Dali paintings, including *Dismal Sport*.)

The painting is, naturally, based on Freudian ideas, including his theory of the persistence of our subconscious, our instinctive nature to manifest itself through conscious expression. By using timepieces as his symbols, Dali is reminding his viewers that our memories serve to consciously catalogue past events. This ability allows our unconscious mind to hold sway over the real world—embodied in the painting by a manmade timepiece—allowing the mind to appear to have some control over time itself.

That three of the watches are melting (*Soft Watches* was another name for the small painting, which only measures 9.5 by 13 inches, or 24 by 33 centimeters) is also symbolic. In Dali's mind, soft objects are unacceptable, even detestable. Soft things are organic; they represent a life and a death; weakness and decay or putrefaction. Compare the droopy watches (none of which has the same time as another) to the rocky beaches of Cadaques. These are solid forms impervious to time, for time has no impact on them or power over them. Although the fourth timepiece, a pocket watch, is not shown drooping, it is swarming with ants, as if it is organic. (Again, a recurring motif of Dali's.) The ants are symbolic of Dali's psychological hangups, including personal anxiousness, and his abhorrence of putrefaction. The pocket watch is also identical to the watch worn by Dali's father in a 1920 portrait, which may symbolize the rotting relationship that then existed between the Spanish painter and his father.

THE POWER OF CHEESE

Even those not familiar with the artwork of Salvador Dali have a general awareness of the melting clocks depicted by the Spanish artist in his work *The Persistence of Memory*. Dali explained the depiction of the droopy images as the result of eating cheese.

He had been working on the canvas and had completed the background, which was yet another depiction of the rocky beachscape of Port Lligat, but the painting's foreground had not yet taken shape in his mind. One evening, Gala and some of their friends made plans to attend the cinema, but Dali chose not to go along, as he was at work on a painting. He had eaten some excellent Camembert cheese, which had turned soft and gooey. The droopy cheese was still on his mind when he returned to the canvas. He had decided to call it a day and put up his brushes and colors; he had a headache—but the Camembert continued to haunt him.

Just as he was preparing for bed, an image came to him. In the same way he kept envisioning the drippy cheese, Dali saw images of melting timepieces. The vision inspired him, and he took up his paints again, even though the hour was late. When Gala and their friends returned a few hours later, Salvador had finished, having added, among other images, four clocks, three of which drooped over other objects in the painting, including a barren tree limb, the edge of a wooden box, and a pinkish, blad-der-like shape. (The fourth clock, a pocket watch, is swarmed by ants, a recurring image in Dali's art.)

Where had the images come from within the mind of Salvador Dali? It was the cheese. In his own words, Dali explained his decision to paint melting clocks: "Be persuaded that Salvador Dali's famous limp watches are nothing but the tender, extravagant and solitary paranoiac-critical Camembert of time and space."* In creating one of his personal masterpieces of surrealist art, Salvador Dali gave credit to the power of cheese.

* Conroy Maddox, *Salvador Dali: Eccentric and Genius* (Cologne, West Germany: Benedikt Tschen Verlag GmbHCo., 1990), 25.

As one of Dali's crowning surrealist paintings, *The Persistence of Memory* became an important work in another way. By early 1932, the painting was on display in the United States as part of an exhibition held at the Julien Levy Gallery in New York City. The painting was included in a retrospective of surrealism, titled "Surrealist Paintings, Drawings, and Photographs." It was through this exhibit and this painting that American art audiences were introduced directly to the works of Salvador Dali.

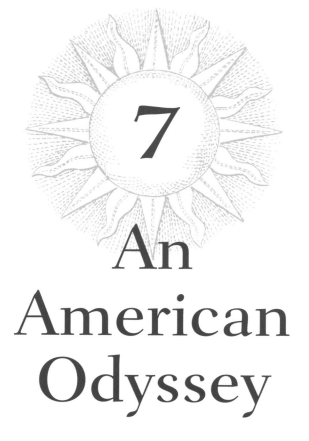

7

An American Odyssey

THE ZODIAC GROUP

By 1933, Dali was still struggling to become an established artist and overcome the skepticism of his audiences in Europe and the United States. That year, he was given his first solo art show, and good reviews outnumbered bad ones. He was not yet entirely popular, however, and buyers were not lining up to purchase his paintings. Again, Gala interceded. She contacted one of the richest art collectors in Europe, Prince Jean-Louis de Faucigny-Lucinge, and proposed a special arrangement for the purchase of Dali's paintings. Twelve patrons were enlisted, each agreeing to support Salvador Dali for one month each year. During each month, Dali was to produce two paintings, one large one and a second, smaller work. With this prearrangement, Dali's painting was commissioned and his income remained constant. Gala and Faucigny-Lucinge gathered 11 supporters (the prince would make 12), who were collectively known as The Zodiac Group. The group included Europeans as well as

Americans, including the American art collector Caresse Crosby, known for her invention of the modern brassiere. The Viscount de Noailles was also one of the 12. This arrangement proved instrumental to the advancement of Dali's career and provided security for years to come. The Zodiac Group continued to commission Dali's work until the outbreak of World War II in 1939.

As for Dali, most of his financial problems soon evaporated, and the 12 supporters helped promote his art. With such support, the value of Dali's paintings increased. Before the year was over, to show his appreciation for the efforts Gala had made on his behalf, Salvador painted a pair of extremely different portraits of Gala, including one that measured less than three by four inches. The other, titled *Sugar Sphinx*, showed a tiny Gala in the painting's bottom foreground, her back to the viewers, pensively contemplating a swirling orange sky of shadow.

In 1934, Dali and Gala were married in a small, civil ceremony. She would remain his constant companion for many decades until their deaths; yet Gala was unfaithful to her artist husband. She even had affairs with her former husband, Paul Éluard. Dali did not appear to mind his wife's indiscretions. He had a lifelong dread or fear of sexual relations with women. Some observers of Dali's relationship with Gala describe both of them as opportunists, each using the other to make certain Dali became a professional and financial success as an artist.

THE ARTIST IN AMERICA

His personal life not withstanding, 1934 brought great rewards for Dali as his career advanced further. He held five solo exhibitions of his work that year, including two in Paris, a third in London, and two others in New York City. (Caresse Crosby helped arrange one of the American shows.) Dali and Gala both took passage onboard the steamer *Champlain*, which crossed the Atlantic to New York in November, the first time either had been to the United States. Since money was still

In 1934, Salvador and Gala Dali visited the United States for the first time, when 22 of Dali's paintings were exhibited in New York. The couple are pictured here shortly after their trans-Atlantic voyage to New York aboard the SS *Champlain*.

limited, Picasso helped pay for their third-class tickets. (At least that is what Dali claimed, although the claim has never been substantiated.) When the couple arrived in New York on the fourteenth, Dali was swarmed by reporters, who had been lined up by Crosby. Dali loved the attention. The Julien Levy

Gallery show (which had hosted a Dali exhibition two years earlier) proved a success. Of the 22 paintings included in the show, 12 sold "at very high prices,"[73] including one to New York's Museum of Modern Art. To celebrate the exhibition, Caresse Crosby and Julien Levy's wife, Joella, hosted the Dalis at a special party on January 18, 1935. It was a costume ball, with each guest dressed as his or her favorite dream. Dali came with his head "neatly bandaged by yards and yards of hospital gauze," whereas Gala attended as a woman "giving birth to a doll from the top of her head."[74]

Dali's time in the United States brought him greater fame and attention in the art world. He enjoyed all the ways that the United States was different from Europe and as his fame was growing, he painted a whimsical work featuring the famous American actress Mae West, *The Face of Mae West (Usable as a Surrealist Apartment)*, which combined elements of her facial features into the landscape of an apartment, including having her trademark platinum hair serve as curtains. A lip-shaped, red couch served as her mouth. (A couple of years later, Dali actually designed a life-size Mae West Lips sofa.) The work is one of Dali's earliest paintings based on humor and whimsy, but there would be others over the years. Having created a buying audience for himself in the United States, he and Gala took passage back to Europe in January onboard the liner *Ile de France*.

Ironically, though, just as Dali was beginning to make a name for himself as a surrealist painter, the surrealists began turning their backs on him. The reasons are complicated. One reason may be that while talking to American reporters, Dali described himself as "the only authentic member of the surrealist movement,"[75] which infuriated his surrealist colleagues in Paris. Dali's comment merely represented the latest in a series of affronts and conflicts between Dali and the surrealist group. In recent years, he had also offended many surrealists through several paintings he had produced.

By the early 1930s, Europe was beginning to feel the impact
(*continued on page 78*)

DALI ON DISPLAY IN NEW YORK

Although Salvador Dali expected his art to be taken seriously in general, there were times when he turned his artistic talents onto projects that were whimsical, intended for a popular audience only. In 1936, during his first visit to New York City, he engaged in one such project, when he agreed to design a window display for a famous department store on New York's Fifth Avenue, Bonwit Teller.

The department store commissioned several surrealist window displays, featuring several different artists, including Dali. It was all part of an attempt to piggy-back on the interest generated that year by Dali's first American exhibit, as well as a special show on surrealism and other avant-garde art forms being held at New York's Museum of Modern Art. Of all the displays, Dali's drew the most attention. Titled "She Was a Surrealist Woman, She Was Like a Figure in a Dream," the Spanish painter included a backdrop of papier-mâché clouds and a female mannequin with a bouquet of red roses in place of her head. Stretching out from tumble-down rubble were long, reddish arms offering her gifts. On a nearby table was a black telephone with a bright orange lobster for a receiver. People lined up six-deep to see the strange display that served in most cases as an introduction to surrealism. The display was a huge publicity stunt and a grand success for Dali.

So when he was asked to design another window display for Bonwit Teller two years later, the Spanish surrealist willingly agreed. In fact, the department store commissioned a pair of windows for Dali. He decided to use the windows to depict the "Narcissus complex." One window would be set in a daytime scene, while the second would depict a night setting. The day scene included an old-time, legged bathtub lined with black Persian lamb's wool and three wax hands holding mirrors emerging from the water in the tub. A late-nineteenth-century wax store mannequin of a woman, dressed in a see-through negligee was depicted about to step into the tub. The female dummy was covered with dust and cobwebs. The night scene featured a bed supported with buffalo legs. Over the bed hung a buffalo head with a dead pigeon in its mouth. Another wax dummy lay on the bed's black satin sheets, as live coals burned beneath her. It was all pure whimsy; all pure Dali.

As hoped, the dual displays drew large crowds. All went well, until the store's management received complaints that the mannequin wearing the filmy negligee was too sexualized. Before the end of the display's first day, store officials ordered the naughty nightie replaced with a tailored suit. The changes may have appeased a scandalized street audience, but Dali was not pleased. When he saw the changed displays, he was outraged and demanded the store restore his original composition. They refused.

Dali then took matters into his own hands. Writing years later, he described what happened next: "So I dashed into the window to disarrange it, so that my name, signed in the window, should not be dishonored. I was never so surprised as when the bath tub just shot through the window when I pushed it and I was thereafter most confused."* Dali and the runaway tub landed on the street. Fortunately, Dali was not hurt when the plate glass window shattered.

Amid a delighted street crowd, thrilled by Dali's antics, New York City police arrived and arrested the Spanish artist, and escorted him to the East 51st Street police station. Within a few hours, Edward James managed to get Dali released, charged only with disorderly conduct. For Dali, the experience was fulfilling. He received endless publicity for his "disorderly conduct," as well as the thrill of getting to spend a few hours in a real New York City jail cell.

* Ian Gibson, *The Shameful Life of Salvador Dali* (New York: W.W. Norton, 1997), 444.

(*continued from page 75*)

of the spread of a right-wing political extremism known as fascism. The National Socialist German Workers Party (the Nazis) leader, Adolf Hitler, had come to power in Germany in January 1933. In Italy, Fascist dictator Benito Mussolini had been ruling with an iron fist since the early 1920s. Many of Dali's fellow surrealists despised the Fascists and aligned themselves with communism, which was "felt to be the moral option to many . . . artists and intellectuals."[76]

As Communist sympathizers, the surrealists held V.I. Lenin (who had died in 1924), the former leader of the Soviet Union, as their political hero. Dali did not share their beliefs in communism, however. Generally, he thought of himself as an artist with few strong political leanings, but his political views leaned toward fascism rather than communism. When Dali chose to include the face of Lenin in two of his paintings, *Evocation of an Appearance of Lenin* (1931) and the *Enigma of William Tell* (1933), he infuriated many surrealists. In the *Evocation*, Dali placed small images of Lenin's face on the keys of a piano. In the *Enigma*, a highly sexualized painting, he gave Tell the face of Lenin. In fact, the William Tell–Lenin painting so angered André Breton, the proclaimed leader of the surrealists, that on February 2, 1934, he tried to destroy the work while it was on display at an exhibition in Paris. The painting was hung so high, however, that he could not reach it. Four days later, Breton summoned Dali to his apartment to account for his anti-communist, anti-Lenin paintings, which Breton described as Dali's "counter-revolutionary acts, tending to the glory of Hitlerian Fascism."[77]

SURREALIST POLITICS

When Dali went to the meeting, he stood before Breton and other assembled surrealists wearing many layers of clothing. (He had caught a cold.) Turning the "trial" into a farce, Dali began taking clothing on and off until he was naked, all the time taking his temperature with a thermometer. His performance amused most of the surrealists, and even Breton had a difficult time keeping a straight face. For the moment, Dali's status among the surrealists was safe, despite Breton's best efforts to have him removed. Dali's days with the surrealists were numbered, however. He was gaining a worldwide reputation; his paintings were selling. Although he would never give up surrealism as an art form, he did distance himself in the future from the Parisian group that had embraced him so enthusiastically just a few years earlier.

Despite his "trial" with Breton and the surrealists, Dali continued to work through 1935, advancing his career even further. He gained a new patron, a wealthy English art collector named Edward James, godson of King Edward VII. The two signed an agreement through which Dali supplied paintings for James to purchase and James would pay Dali monthly just for the right to purchase any works of his choice. This lucrative arrangement continued for a decade. Today, the Edward James Foundation's collection of surrealist works is one of the most extensive anywhere.

Through such millionaire benefactors as Edward James, the Dalis began to move in an elite circle, the "smart set," which included wealthy business tycoons and old-money aristocrats. Salvador and Gala became the darlings of the social circles in Paris and beyond. They were wined and dined, and invited to frequent parties and weekends where Dali enjoyed lavish hospitality. He came to envy the lifestyles of the rich and famous.

Dali never allowed much time to pass between his writings, and that year he published *The Conquest of the Irrational*. The book further described his "paranoiac-critical method" of composing and painting his canvases. Dali also gave lectures on the subject. At the same time, he was experimenting with a new form of surrealism, which is embodied in a series of paintings inspired by mid-nineteenth-century French artist Jean-François Millet's work, *The Angelus*. The Millet painting is a simple, realistic composition featuring a farm couple standing in a field, praying. Dali, of course, took the painting and its

Nineteenth-century French artist Jean-François Millet's work, *The Angelus*, which depicts a peasant couple praying in a field at sunset, inspired Dali to produce a series of paintings that built on Millet's theme. Among these works is *The Architectonic Angelus of Millet* (pictured here), which Dali painted in 1933.

pietistic subject and turned it into a study of such themes as the "castration of the husband and the killing of the son."[78] (Despite the fact that there is no son pictured in the Millet painting, Dali insisted that an X-ray of the painting would reveal a small casket lying between the farm couple, which

Millet later painted over with a basket. Of course, Millet painted nothing of the sort.)

In one of Dali's versions of *The Angelus*, the couple became symbols of the struggle between the sexes, and he turns the pair into praying mantises, an insect whose mating ritual is completed by the female killing the male. (Although the painting recasts the pair as stone towers, Dali writes about his praying mantis transformation in a book that was not published until 1963, because the manuscript became lost during the 1930s.) Death is also symbolized by the cypress trees that surround the two stone figures. Here is a classic example of Dali's "paranoia-critical method." In the painting, he has depicted his strong, personal fear of female sexuality. He would return to this subject later in 1935 through another painting, *Woman with a Head of Roses*.

MAKING A SPLASH

Dali continued to gain notoriety as a flamboyant, exhibitionist-driven surrealist. In 1936, he made a splash in London, where he was invited to present a lecture at the International Surrealist Exhibition that summer. (Breton and Paul Éluard delivered lectures, as well.) The exhibition opened in late July, with 2,000 people in attendance. There were more than 400 paintings, drawings, sculptures, and other art pieces on display by 68 artists, including three paintings by Dali: *The Dream, Daybreak,* and *Paranoiac Head.* Fourteen countries were represented at the summer exhibition. The outrageous artist showed up wearing a deep-sea diving suit and lead boots. He gave his speech in this madcap attire, making the point that he was "diving" into his unconscious. Had it not been for Edward James, who managed to remove Dali's diving helmet in the nick of time, he would have suffocated in his enclosed suit.

The exhibition in London was quickly followed by an extremely successful solo show in the British capital at the gallery of Alex, Reid, and Lefevre; it included 29 paintings and 18 drawings. Seven of Dali's paintings sold there, even before the show opened. By noon on the exhibition's opening day, Dali had sold ten paintings and five drawings. "Surrealism is catching on wonderfully in London,"[79] Dali told a friend.

THE SPANISH CIVIL WAR

Dali and Gala were still in London, staying at Edward James'

THE OTHER PAINTER FROM CATALONIA

During Salvador Dali's lengthy career as a painter, sculptor, and writer, he became known as one of the most famous men from his native Catalonia; certainly the most famous surrealist. Dali was not the only noteworthy artist from his home region, however. Another was his contemporary, yet his elder by nearly 20 years, Joan Miró.

Dali's fellow Catalan was raised on a farm outside Barcelona and was extremely proud of his Catalan heritage. He arrived on the art scene in Paris in 1919, at the end of World War I, but often returned to Catalonia, usually to spend summers with his father, working on the family farm.

Within a few years of his arrival in Paris, Miró became one of the early leaders of the surrealist group. He included his name in the group's founding document, the *Surrealist Manifesto*, and his support of the group's ideals remained a constant throughout his life. As with many of the early surrealists, Miró's art was not immediately popular, and he sold few paintings. Like several of his fellow artists, he experienced great poverty and sometimes nearly starved to death. He claimed that one of his early paintings was the result of "my hallucinations brought on by hunger."*

Miró and Dali's career in the world of surrealist art overlapped more than once. It was Miró who encouraged Dali at an early age to hone his skills with paints and brush. Impressed during a visit to Dali's studio in 1927, Miró wrote to him later, stating: "You are without a doubt a very gifted artist with a home on Wimpole Street, when they received news from Spain. The long-awaited outbreak of the Spanish Civil War had taken place. The 1930s were marred by an economic depression that swept through Europe and the other nations of the industrialized West. With serious economic problems everywhere, political extremism was taking root both in certain

brilliant career ahead of you—in Paris!"** Dali was equally impressed with Miró's art. The following year, in writing a review of an exhibition of Miró's surrealist works, he penned these lines: "Miró returns the line, dot, . . . and colors to their pure, elemental, magical possibilities . . . Miró's art is too big for the stupid world of our artists and intellectuals."*** When Dali went to Paris, a young man of 25, he was introduced to the surrealist group by Miró, who was in his mid-40s and already well-established as an artist. In later years, after both Dali and Miró had made their names in the art world, they held a joint exhibition of their works at the Museum of Modern Art in New York City.

Although both of these native-born Catalans proved themselves extraordinary artists, they were extremely different men in temperament and personality. Dali was outgoing and flamboyant, and loved the spotlight, whereas Miró was a quiet, reserved man, one who was extremely modest and stayed out of the public eye. They did not view politics in the same way, either. During the Spanish Civil War, Miró supported the Republicans, whereas Dali remained publicly neutral. Beyond such differences, though, Salvador Dali and Joan Miró pursued their art with a spirit of independence that was reflected in their shared heritage, not only as native-born Spaniards but as Catalans.

* Robert Anderson, *Salvador Dali* (Danbury, Conn.: Franklin Watts, 2002), 42.
** Ibid.
*** Ibid.

European capitals, and beyond, in countries such as Japan. In 1933, German Fascist leader Adolf Hitler came to power and brought down the struggling, fledgling Weimar Republic, which Hitler replaced with National Socialism (the Nazis). In Italy, Fascist dictator Benito Mussolini had come to power in the 1920s. Now it was Spain's turn. In 1931, the Spanish people had overthrown royal rule and established yet another shaky democracy, the Second Republic. For five years, the Spanish government had struggled against rival powers, such as the aristocratic landowners, industrialists, the Catholic Church, and its military. It would be the military that would finally challenge the existence of the Republic. By the spring of 1936, new Spanish elections resulted in the formation of a coalition government that gave voice to political extremist groups, including Communists and Socialists. The new government proved unpopular and, in July, a band of renegade army officers, led by General Francisco Franco, revolted against the Popular Front. By late September, the rebel army laid siege to the government in Madrid. On October 1, Franco declared himself the head of the Spanish government. To add to the controversy, Franco's Fascist forces would receive support and aid from other Fascists, including Hitler's Nazis and Mussolini's Black Shirts. For three years, civil war would tear Spain apart.

After returning briefly to Spain, Dali and Gala decided to leave again, uncertain of the war's outcome. Following their departure from Port Lligat, their house was ransacked, and Dali's family home in Cadaques was bombed and partially damaged. Suddenly, Dali and Gala were nomads bent on escaping the threat of civil war. The couple returned to Paris in late 1936, then left France in September 1937 and took up residence in Italy, where they would stay in another of Edward James' estate homes, along with fashion designer Coco Chanel.

Meanwhile, the war brought personal tragedy. Federico Garcia Lorca, Dali's old friend, was captured and killed by Franco's forces, and Dali's sister, Ana Maria, was also captured and tortured, scarring her for life. Even in the face of these events, however, Dali refused to take sides in the civil war. Most other Spanish painters, such as Picasso and Joan Miró, threw their support to the Republicans. (Picasso, of course, would paint one of his greatest works, a large mural called *Guernica*, in protest of the Fascist bombing of the small, undefended Basque town of the same name.) Dali continued to remain neutral, however, even after Lorca was killed.

In Italy, Dali and Gala attempted to live a normal life. They toured the country and took in the sights, but it was a difficult period for Dali. The war seems to have brought on some form of nervous exhaustion, which required him to take a long bed rest in Cortina. After his recovery, however, he was revitalized artistically, having gained a new appreciation for the works of the Italian Renaissance, as well as the Baroque period. Because of his increasing popularity as an artist, Dali was also becoming a popular cultural icon. He created advertisements based on some of his surrealist themes for American magazines, such as *Harper's Bazaar, Vogue,* and *Town and Country*. For a time, he worked with the American comedians the Marx Brothers on a scene for a film titled *Giraffes on Horseback Salad*. But the project never panned out.

War
and Exile

PROTESTING WAR

By 1939, the Fascists under General Franco's leadership had won the Spanish Civil War and established a dictatorship. Although Dali did not immediately support Franco, later in life he would change his mind. As for the war itself, Dali was saddened and angered by the devastation it had caused. At least 500,000 Spaniards died in the conflict, some the victims of support given to Franco by Italy's Benito Mussolini and the Nazi leader Adolf Hitler. Two of Dali's paintings reflect his disgust with the civil conflict—*Autumn Cannibalism* and *Soft Construction with Boiled Beans: Premonition of Civil War*. Both were painted in 1936.

His *Cannibalism* painting depicts a couple who are entwined in surrealistic ways while engaged in a meal. The figures symbolize Dali's images of cannibalism and civil war. As the man and woman eat, they "scoop the flesh of the other with knife and spoon as they embrace: a sexually violent personification of a country at war with

During the mid-to-late 1930s, Salvador Dali incorporated many of Austrian psychotherapist Sigmund Freud's (pictured here) concepts into his artwork. One such concept was displacement, which Dali represented by painting drawers in the anatomy of his human subjects.

itself."[80] Dali's *Soft Construction* features a deconstructed grotesque human figure that appears as both male and female. Head is connected to leg; torso connected to hands—all in a depiction of the Spanish Civil War. Because Dali painted the work before the war had fully broken out, he later added his secondary title: *Premonition of Civil War*. (There appear to be questions about whether the work was intended originally to

(*continued on page 90*)

DALI MEETS FREUD

Although Salvador Dali relied on many sources of inspiration for his art (including his surrealism), one source may have influenced him more than any other. His paintings were often expressions of psychological "hang-ups," so in them Dali was expressing theories he had discovered in the writings of the father of psychoanalysis, Sigmund Freud. In 1938, the two men would meet.

That spring, on March 11, the German Nazi leader Adolf Hitler completed the annexation of neighboring Austria, Freud's homeland. Within a week, rumors reached Paris that the Nazis had arrested Freud. The surrealists, led by Breton, publicly protested this unnecessary treatment of the elderly Austrian. Most likely, the Germans did not actually arrest Freud, but chose instead to keep him under close surveillance. Freud, after all, was one of the most prominent Jews in Vienna.

Fortunately, the 79-year-old Freud and his daughter, Anna, were able to escape Vienna. They reached Paris, then proceeded on to London, arriving there on June 6. Refugee father and daughter took up residence with a friend, Stefan Zweig, who was also Jewish and living in exile in London. When his idol surfaced in England, Dali was interested in meeting him.

Dali had long considered Freud and his fellow, but older, Spanish artist Picasso to be father figures. He had met Picasso several times and often spoke of the cubist painter as a close friend, which they really were not. Salvador had tried several times to visit Freud in Vienna in earlier years but had never been successful.

Fortunately, not only was Stefan Zweig a friend of Edward James, Dali's most recent major patron, but he was also a great admirer of Dali. The Spanish artist asked James for Zweig's address. After receiving a series of letters from Dali asking to see Freud, Zweig responded. He spoke to the ailing Freud, telling him how Dali was "the most faithful and most grateful disciple of your ideas among the artists."* He told Freud that Dali wanted to show him his latest painting, *Metamorphosis of Narcissus*. Freud agreed to give Dali an audience.

The meeting took place on July 19, 1938. Little is known of the details. Since Dali did not speak German or English, the two men probably spoke to one another in French. Freud allowed Dali to sketch a portrait of him. For both men, it appears, the meeting went well and each was impressed by the other. For Dali, the encounter "was undoubtedly one of the most important experiences of his life."**

Dali made a distinct impression on Freud, who had not kept up with the surrealist movement for several years. What he did know, he had largely dismissed. After meeting Dali, however, he came away with a different view. In writing a letter to Zweig the day after Dali's visit, the aged psychoanalyst penned complimentary words for the Spanish painter:

> I have to thank you indeed for the introduction of our visitor of yesterday. Until now I was inclined to regard the Surrealists—who seem to have adopted me as their patron saint—as 100 per cent fools . . . This young Spaniard, with his ingenuous fanatical eyes, and his undoubtedly technically perfect mastership, has suggested to me a different estimate.***

And what did Freud think of the painting Dali showed him during their encounter? With the eye of a true psychiatrist, Freud gave his analysis. Of the painting, he wrote that there "are serious problems from the psychological point of view."†

* Ian Gibson, *The Shameful Life of Salvador Dali* (New York: W.W. Norton, 1997), 437.
** Ibid., 439.
*** Ibid., 438.
† Ibid.

(*continued from page 87*)

portray the war or not.) The surrounding landscape is barren, stripped of all life, and the sky is heavy with contrasting clouds and colors, heavenly signs of the disaster that is about to unfold in Dali's native land. As for the boiled beans, they are meant to symbolize poverty and food shortages.

During the mid-to-late 1930s, Dali began experimenting with a new surrealist symbolism. In an attempt to depict yet another aspect of Freud's ideas—this time displacement—Dali painted several pictures, often of human figures, with various drawers built into their anatomy. With this device, the painter transforms his figures into "architectural metaphors of memory and of the unconscious mind."[81] Through this method, the drawers become symbols of various desires, needs, and impulses, while graphically presenting a clear picture to the viewer. One such painting is *The Burning Giraffe*, which he created between 1936 and 1937. A female-like figure, lithe and wearing a filmy piece of clothing, sports one drawer just below her breasts, while her left leg is decorated with seven drawers all placed in a row. Dali intended the drawers as symbols.

In another such work, *Spain* (1938), Dali combines two of his surrealist techniques—his symbolic drawers and his double-images technique, the optical illusion known as *trompes l'oeil*. (The previous year, Dali had created one of his finest examples of this illusory imaging in his *Metamorphosis of Narcissus*, the painting Dali took on his visit with Freud.) The woman's face doubles as people fighting. Her breasts become a pair of knights carrying lances. The woman is depicted leaning on a nightstand. (This time, the drawers are not an extension of a human directly, but there is still symbolism aplenty.) The night stand represents the Spanish Civil War and the bloody scarf hanging from the opened drawer depicts the destructive nature of war.

Even as the Spanish Civil War came to an end in 1939, though, another war, also driven by fascism, began. In early September, following the German invasion of Poland, Great Britain and France declared war on the Nazi aggressors. Soon,

World War II was under way, and it would become the largest war in history. In another two years, the Soviet Union and the United States would enter the international conflict.

World War II would be a war that Dali would not be able to ignore or escape. Ultimately, the war and its aftermath would have dramatic effects on the Spanish painter's art. Although Freud had served as an inspiration for all surrealists, including Dali, Salvador gradually found himself moving away from Freudian ideas in his art. Although he had managed to visit Freud while he was in exile in England, the Viennese psychoanalyst had not been terribly supportive of him and, during the visit, was largely detached. After all, he never had a full understanding of what the surrealists were trying to accomplish. (Freud would die just a year after Dali's visit, so he never had the opportunity to learn about Dali's symbolism.) Still obsessed, but rejecting Freud as he had been rejected, Dali sought other inspirations. World War II did not inspire the Spaniard much while it was being fought, but he was mesmerized by the development of the atomic bomb, as well as nuclear physics. In addition, he found new inspirations in Catholicism, the religion of his mother and of his early years.

Not only did Dali generally reject Freud and his theories by the early 1940s, but the surrealist group, still under the leadership of Breton, rejected the controversial and outspoken Spanish artist. Throughout his life, Dali's politics leaned to the right and away from the left-leaning ideology of communism. (His earlier, mocking depictions of Lenin in his art had infuriated the surrealists.) As Germany spread its aggression across Europe, the Fascist-Nazi leader Adolf Hitler became a despised symbol to the left in general and the surrealists specifically. Although Dali was never a true advocate of Hitler, he wrote that he thought the German dictator was "interesting, even attractive, from a Surrealist point of view."[82] This rankled the surrealists, who would not tolerate anything short of absolute condemnation of Hitler and the Nazis. After the publication of his controversial opinions in an essay, the surrealists expelled

Dali from their group. All formal ties between Dali and the avant-garde group led by Breton were completely severed.

ESCAPING THE WAR

In general, the war represented years of upheaval for Dali and Gala. They remained in Paris until the Germans seemed to be on the brink of marching into the city itself. They fled to Font Romeu and then Arcachon, north of Bordeaux, where other artists, including the great cubist painter Marcel Duchamp, lived as refugees. In 1940, when the Nazis did invade, Dali and Gala escaped from France, but much of Dali's most recently completed artwork was left behind and thus lost or destroyed. The war had already impacted Dali's work, as seen in his paintings *Telephone in a Dish with Three Grilled Sardines at the End of September* (1939), *Daddy Longlegs of the Evening—Hope!* (1940), and *The Face of War*. The first was a stark painting of two halves—both a still life and an eerie, remote landscape in the background. The painting was intended to depict—symbolically, of course—telephone conversations between Hitler and British Prime Minister Neville Chamberlain in 1938, which resulted in the handing over of part of Czechoslovakia by the British and French to Germany. (Dali had painted a work with a similar "telephone" theme—*The Enigma of Hitler*—in 1939.) Of the German Nazi Party leader, Dali once wrote: "If Hitler were to ever conquer Europe, he would do away with hysterics of my kind . . . Hitler interested me purely as a focus for my own mania and because he struck me as having an unequaled disaster value."[83]

Daddy Longlegs "is a depressing, haunting work that trumpets the evils and carnage of war."[84] The work includes elements of his "melting" symbols first used in his painting *The Persistence of Memory*, with its droopy timepieces. One of the figures depicted in *The Persistence of Memory* and *Dismal Sport* is used in this painting, as well—the amoeba-like head that represents a self-portrait. The artist's head is lifeless, a symbol of "the destruction of art and beauty."[85] Other artistic symbols are present, including a deflated cello (music) and inkwells (the literary arts). A cannon stands menacingly at the painting's left. But in the midst of despair and destruction, Dali has included a daddy longlegs crawling along the artist's face, its shadow creating the shape of a flower, the painting's reference to hope.

Throughout much of 1940, Dali and Gala wandered in search of a place of peace and security. They went to Madrid (Spain was neutral during World War II, and the Spanish Civil War was over), and Dali took a side trip to visit his family in Cadaques, where he paid a call on his father and Ana Maria, his sister. He also visited his bombed-out home at Port Lligat and was stunned at the devastation he found, not only there but throughout much of his native Spain. Gala had already left for Lisbon to buy tickets for an ocean liner voyage to the United States. To meet up with her there, Dali took his first airplane trip, from Madrid to Lisbon, although he had a lifelong fear of flying. From there, they took passage to the United States onboard the ship *Excambion*, of the American Export Line. When the couple arrived in New York on August 16, 1940, Dali met with eager reporters. By this time, he was a worldwide phenomenon. The curious—both art lovers and others—wanted to hear what this latest refugee from the European war had to say. He did not disappoint them. He informed the American press that surrealism was no longer a living art form and that he was about to create a new style in its place. Dali and Gala had arrived in the United States to escape the ravage and threats of a war inspired by fascism. They would not return to Europe for another eight years.

Dali and Gala moved about in the States, visiting friends. They stayed for a while in Hampton Manor, an old plantation mansion in Virginia and the home of Caresse Crosby. (The American writer Henry Miller and the Castilian novelist Anais Nin were also visiting at the time. Miller was not impressed by Dali, and Nin did not like Gala.) Dali and Gala also visited Edward James, who owned a home in Taos, New Mexico. They even lived in California for a time, spending the summer of 1941 at the Del Monte Lodge, in Pebble Beach. They would return there over the next several years, and the luxurious resort became known as their American Port Lligat.

For a time, they returned to live at Hampton Manor, where Dali worked on one of his most important writings, *Secret Life*, an overwritten autobiography in which he claims to have salvaged modern art from abstraction and recaptured earlier, realist traditions from art history. Toward the end of his memoir, he also claimed to be in the midst of "seeking reconciliation with the Catholic Church."[86] (The book was published in 1942.) After hopping from coast to coast, Dali and Gala returned to New York, where they took up residence at the stately St. Regis Hotel, a few blocks from the Museum of Modern Art.

By 1941, New York's Museum of Modern Art held Dali's first retrospective exhibition, which included 50 paintings, 17 drawings, and 6 pieces of jewelry. During the exhibit, which ran from November 1941 until January 11, 1942, the United States entered World War II, following Japan's bombing of Hawaii's Pearl Harbor. The exhibit was sent on tour to eight American cities. The press was always interested in Dali, and he was featured in various American magazines, including *Life*. He found time to paint and created *Soft Self-Portrait with Grilled Bacon* (1941), which was an homage of sorts to America's love affair with bacon. As for Dali's portrait, it was supported by nine crutches, a symbol he had used in earlier surrealist paintings. As he had also done in earlier paintings, he included ants.

Two years later, he painted another work that recognized the importance of his new home, his new art, and America's place in the New World—*Geopoliticus Child Watching the Birth of the New Man*. Although the work was allegorical, its symbolism was straightforward; it steered clear of much of the intellectual symbolism of surrealism. In this work, the "New Man" is obviously the United States, as it is hatching from an egg. (The egg is a globe, showing the continents.) A withered female is shown representing the Old World (Europe). There is little here to remind viewers of Freud or Dali's old paranoiac-critical style. He had turned, or perhaps returned, to a straight-on, representational style of classical art.

BOOKS, FILMS, AND ATOMS

During the 1940s, the years he spent in the United States, Dali gained a guarded affection for the country. He was selling paintings and making money, and the popular culture attracted him. Once Gala realized that they could make money by connecting Dali's name with commercial products, he took on projects intended to provide publicity for everything from body oils to women's hosiery. He also agreed to provide illustration for dozens of newly published books, including Maurice Sandoz's *Fantastic Memories* and Billy Rose's *Wine, Women, and Words*, as well as reprints of classical works such as *Don Quixote* and Shakespeare's *Macbeth*. He also designed stage sets and ballet costumes, as Picasso had earlier in his own career.

By 1945, Dali was again working in film, but this time it was not on a cutting-edge surrealist project. In the fall of 1945, the great movie director Alfred Hitchcock hired Dali to create a scene depicting a nightmare for a feature film, *Spellbound*, which starred Gregory Peck and Ingrid Bergman. The scene designed by Dali depicted a ballroom with more than a dozen pianos suspended from the ceiling. But Dali's imagined sequence proved beyond the movie studio's budget and the scene was not included in Hitchcock's film. A few months later, another Hollywood studio mogul called Dali, wanting him to help design drawings for a short film titled *Destino*. The film was to run only six minutes and would comprise several short episodes, what Disney called a "package film." This project, too, did not come to fruition. Walt Disney decided to scrap the project when he became convinced the film was not marketable.

In 1945, Alfred Hitchcock (pictured here) hired Salvador Dali to create a series of eerie dream sequences for his movie *Spellbound*. Although only a few of Dali's scenes made the final cut for the movie, his fame continued to grow in the United States.

Although such projects failed, Dali's fame continued to grow both in the United States and around the world. Even as he worked on his failed collaboration with Hitchcock, Dali's paintings were being displayed in an exhibition at the Bignou Gallery in New York City. The titles of Dali's paintings were always odd-sounding and metaphysical, but among his paintings at the Bignou exhibit (held from late November through

December 1945), one had an intriguing twentieth-century title—*Atomica Melancholica*. Three months earlier, an event of historical impact brought on, not only the end of the war with Japan in the Pacific but a new era of the twentieth century. To end the war with Japan, during the first week of August, the United States dropped a pair of atomic bombs on the cities of Hiroshima and Nagasaki. The twin detonations killed nearly a quarter-million people. The use of atomic weapons brought about an abrupt end to the war, and it would also change the nature of future global conflicts.

This new "atomic" world had a clear impact on Salvador Dali: He would later write: "The atomic explosion of 6 August 1945 shook me seismically. . . . Thenceforth, the atom was my favorite food for thought. Many of the landscapes painted in this period express the great fear inspired in me by the announcement of that explosion."[87] The world's, as well as Dali's, atomic age was about to begin. It would be his last.

A World of
New Realities

NUCLEAR MYSTICISM

Although the atomic blasts detonated on the Japanese cities of
Hiroshima and Nagasaki in early August 1945 would take Dali's art
in new directions, other impulses and motivations also redirected
his creativity during the following decades. As he had already wrote
about in his 1942 memoir, *Secret Life*, he was to largely abandon surrealism and turn to a new form of realism, one less cluttered with his
odd fantasies and strange symbols based on Freudian theory. Freud
would cease to be an inspiration for Dali's art; instead, he turned to
another scientist, Dr. Werner Heisenberg, a contemporary physicist,
for his source of enlightenment.

He would include the world of neutrons and electrons in his
1952 painting *Galatea of the Spheres*. In this work, he returned to a
form of his earlier "double images," this time by creating a portrait
of Gala's face through a series of circular atomic particles. He would

Salvador Dali—pictured here in 1980, nine years prior to his death—abandoned surrealism after World War II. The eccentric artist instead focused on several new themes, including atomic theory, physics, and Catholicism.

also find redirection in his art through the rediscovery of religion and the Catholic Church. Just as nuclear physics was the source of energy for the physical world, so mysticism—through the Catholic Church—would provide the power of faith. Through this combination of inspirations, Dali developed his theory of "nuclear mysticism." Over the next 20 years, he wrote articles, as he had in the past while a surrealist, explaining this approach to his art. To mark the death of his surrealist style, he painted, between 1952 and 1954, *The Disintegration of the Persistence of Memory*. In this work, he deconstructs his famous eerie landscape dominated by melting timepieces, breaking down the symbolic parts of the work into fragments and particles of solid objects. He creates a canvas in which nuclear physics replaces the dreaming landscape, once colorful but now hiding "a vast under girding of floating blocks and spores."[88] His 1931 painting had been about the subconscious and the metaphysical landscape of the mind, but this new work was about the portrayal of physical matter.

Dali's post–World War II themes—atomic theory and physics, Catholicism, the abandonment of surrealists—took the Spanish painter in new directions. During the war, he had turned 50 years old. He would live nearly four more decades, and he was not yet finished creating new art for a new age—the atomic age.

After eight years in the United States, in 1948, Dali finally returned to his native Spain. (Dali and Gala's house at Port Lligat, which had been partially destroyed during the Spanish Civil War, had been rebuilt during their absence.) Having redefined himself, he returned to his homeland, which he had desperately missed. Amid the changes in his art was his nearly complete separation from any further influence by Picasso. He had often worked in his fellow Spaniard's shadow. Over the years, because of Picasso's huge popularity and his general impact on modern art, Dali had been led to mimic his rival's various styles. He would do so no longer. In 1947, before returning to Spain, Dali created a painting, *Portrait of Picasso*, which mocked the elder Spanish artist's "pursuit of ugliness and intellectualism in his paintings."[89] The painting features Picasso's face in profile sporting satyr's horns, his eye sockets hollow, and his brains sticking out of his mouth, forming into a spoon. In the spoon is a guitar, a recurring motif in several important Picasso paintings, especially his cubist paintings. In so many ways, Dali returned to Europe after his American exile a changed artist.

When he did return to Spain, he was criticized for his support of Francisco Franco, who ruled his homeland as a strongman dictator. Although Spain's economy was being destroyed and its culture hampered by restrictions of the right-wing regime, Dali became a full-fledged supporter of Franco. His personal politics had always leaned to the right rather than the left; and it was important to Dali that he be able to return to Spain and work without interference from the government, even though the Franco regime had been responsible for the deaths of hundreds of thousands of Spaniards, including his friend, Lorca.

With the approach of the 1950s, Dali was as famous as he had ever been. He was known for his strange art, his extraordinarily long mustache (in 1954, he even wrote a book about his mustache), and his walking cane, which he began to carry around when he was a teenager. He had already published another book, *Fifty Secrets of Magic Craftsmanship*, in which he once more informed the public of his intent to "return to classicism with renewed vigor."[90] He was also wealthy; his paintings selling at premium prices. Dali had become, to the art-consuming public, the great artist he had always assumed he was. Upon his return to Spain, he paid a visit to Cadaques, where he reconnected with his father and his sister, Ana Maria. To some extent, father and son came to terms with one another. Dali's father had remarried, he was quite elderly, and he wanted to see his son again. After their prolonged visit, Dali wrote to his father: "First of all, thank you for your hospitality. In the few days spent at your side I found my affection for you growing as much as my admiration for your great personality."[91] He ended the note: "Lots of kisses for 'Tieta' [Dali's stepmother, as well as his aunt] and for all of you the affection of your son who loves you."[92]

MYSTICISM AND FAITH

With the awful scope of World War II now in the past, Dali set a new course for himself, both professionally and personally. Following the war, he turned increasingly toward the power of faith, religion, and to the Catholic Church in general. Raised by an atheist father and a devout Catholic mother, Dali had never taken the Church seriously as an adult, and religion and faith had rarely been a subject of his painting, except on those occasions when he mocked religion. By the late 1940s, the Spanish painter began to take religion, especially the role of mysticism, more personally. Since mystics often rely on visions as religious experiences that draw them closer to God, Dali believed that mysticism was a type of surrealist expression, one that focused on the unconscious mind.

There was more to Dali's greater reliance on matters of faith than simply for metaphysical expression, however. He was turning to the Catholic Church itself. In 1949, he made the first of two visits to Rome to see Pope Pius XII. In Rome, he studied religious art closely. He reconnected with Spanish artists such as Velázquez and Zurbaran, who had painted religious subjects in the seventeenth century. He had been reading the works of Jesuit theologian Pierre Teilhard de Chardin, whose ideas concerning religion fascinated Dali, even though they were, at the time, controversial. Then, his father died in 1950. All these influences drew Dali into the realm of the spiritual, and his paintings soon included religious subjects, including several focusing on Christ's Crucifixion. In 1951, he painted the technically stunning *Christ of St. John on the Cross.*

Not the St. John of the New Testament, this John was a Spaniard who lived during the 1500s and was said to have had a vision of Jesus suspended in the air. (Dali claimed to have been inspired by a dream in which Jesus was characterized by the nucleus of an atom. In Dali's mind, the Christ-like nucleus represented "the very unity of the universe."[93]) In Dali's painting, the viewer looks down, as if from Heaven, toward Earth with a scene of the Crucifixion floating in space. At the bottom of the painting is a calm seascape rimmed by the rocks of Cadaques. This painting was Dali's attempt to portray "the most beauty and joy of anything anyone has painted up to the present day."[94]

The redirecting of Dali's art led him to paint grand canvases filled with the spectacle of significant historical events. Although he no longer called the United States his home, he still painted using the New World as his subject matter. One such painting was his *The Discovery of America by Christopher Columbus*, a giant canvas standing more than 13 feet high. Just as Dali had spent his recent years living between Spain and the United States, this painting manages to pay homage to both one of the greatest heroes of Spanish history (even though he was a Genoan, from Italy) and the lands he "discovered," opening them to both exploration and colonization. Dali included Gala in the painting as a saintly muse to Columbus, the innocent seeker. (Dali included himself in the painting as an aged, kneeling Carmelite monk.) Another larger-than-life history painting is his *Santiago el Grande*. An homage work to his Spanish homeland, the painting portrays the patron saint of Spain, St. James of Compostela. Although the work is straightforward, it does not appear without symbols; one section shows the saint "charging on his horse beneath four jasmine petals that burst into a creative atomic cloud."[95] Both the Columbus work and the St. James portrait include views of the floating Crucifixion that Dali first used in *St. John of the Cross*.

DALI AND GALA

During these years of redirection in Dali's art, he and Gala continued to live side by side, spending time almost each year between Paris, New York, and their perpetual home, their house at Port Lligat. They lived extravagantly while in the two great capitals of culture, for they had become part of a crowd of wealthy, fun-seeking jet-setters. This only left Dali time to paint at Port Lligat. His newly found interest in religion and mysticism led him to visit the pope a second time in 1955. By

1958, he and Gala recommitted their marriage, this time in a Catholic church. But, despite this renewal of their vows, Gala remained unfaithful to Dali. Theirs was never a sexual relationship, and she had constant male companions. Although Dali always denied that these distractions of Gala's bothered him personally, he was not happy with their relationship.

As Gala grew older, she wanted more and more material wealth. She spent a fortune on her constant liaisons with men. Dali, during one of their many arguments, once accused her: "You've wasted a fortune on your boys!"[96] Although, by the 1960s, Dali was worth $10 million (today, that amount would probably be more than $200 million), she continually pushed him to paint to support her extravagant lifestyle. She was never satisfied financially or socially. There would be times when she would lock him up in his studio, refusing to allow him out until he had painted that day.

By the early 1960s, she insisted he buy her a castle to live in. He obliged, purchasing Castle Púbol, situated between Figueres and Barcelona. Gala remained so tightfisted about their finances that, in 1964, when the city of Figueres began building a museum to honor Dali, she refused to allow him to donate any of his pictures. The aging painter gave up some of his works anyway. Gala's behavior became more erratic with age. She began to abuse Dali physically. Whenever he did anything to displease her, she would become angry and attack him, taking her hands and scratching his face with her rings. Despite such behavior on Gala's part, he remained loyal to her until her death. He had, after all, engaged in his own self-absorbed behavior all his life, and he was reputed to have physically abused her, as well. As Dali and Gala aged, they struggled with their relationship. She took residence in her castle, continuing her long string of male relationships and requiring Dali to make a formal written request every time he wanted to see her.

Although Dali remained in the public eye through the 1960s and 1970s, his star was beginning to fade. He was becoming a curious old man whose life had been spent doing even more curious things. He began to have trouble using his hands by the late 1970s. Doctors diagnosed him with Parkinson's disease, which slowly causes nerve damage. He also suffered anxiety attacks, mostly brought on by Gala's unguarded and selfish behaviors.

There were still honors and exhibitions, and, in 1974, Dali's new Theater-Museum opened in Figueres. It was the year of his seventieth birthday. He was given awards from around the world. A major retrospective of his body of work was held in France at the Centre Georges Pompidou in 1979. Before the end of the year, the Académie Française enlisted him into its ranks. Already, however, Dali was struggling with poor health, having undergone prostate surgery the previous year. Two years later, the king of Spain, Juan Carlos, and Queen Sofia visited Dali at his home in Port Lligat to pay their respects to the aging Spanish master. Between Gala's separation from him and his poor health, Salvador Dali was beginning to lose his will to create, as well as his lust for life. Dali's psychoanalyst, Dr. Pierre Roumeguère, summed up the situation in a 1980 interview:

> The truth is that Dali no longer wishes to live. He is seventy-six. That he has Parkinson's disease is certain, but what's happening here is an auto suicide—quite simply because Gala is no longer concerned with him. When she is not "wandering" she brutalizes, bullies, and insults Dali as much as possible.[97]

Then, in 1982, Gala suddenly and unexpectedly died. She had become the victim of dementia. Despite the difficulties of their last several years together, Dali mourned her passing with great emotion. They had been together since 1929. He never recovered from the loss of his longtime companion. Shortly after Gala's death, King Juan Carlos granted an aristocratic title on Salvador Dali, who would become Marques de Dali de Púbol. But the honor meant little to the suffering Dali without Gala by his side. His final years were extremely difficult. He

Prince Felipe of Spain is pictured here standing next to one of Salvador Dali's paintings during an exhibition in Barcelona in 2004, entitled "Dali, Mass Culture." The exhibition celebrated the 100th anniversary of the birth of one of modern art's most renowned artists.

continued to produce artistically for one year after Gala's death, but he had not produced any significant works of art since the late 1970s. His final painting was *The Swallow's Tail*.

During his final years, still fascinated with the latest innovations in science, he began to experiment with holograms. Among his final works was an exhibition of holograms displayed in New York. As he continued to age, he constantly battled illness, and he suffered severe burns on his hands when an accidental fire broke out in Castle Púbol, where he remained out of sight, even refusing to see his old friends. Then, on January 23, 1989, Salvador Dali died at the age of 84.

AN ARTIST'S LEGACY

What, then, may be said of the long evolution of Salvador Dali's artistic career? Was he the genius of modern art that he always claimed to be? Had he managed to create something worth remembering—an approach to painting, drawing, and sculpting that significantly influenced twentieth-century art? The answer to these questions must be a resounding *yes*. But what had he done with his art? How had he accomplished his purposes as a painter? What had he meant by painting strange collections of symbols, many of which were disturbing and often incomprehensible? The question is easy to pose, the answer complicated.

Salvador Dali is, undoubtedly, one of the most popular and easily recognized painters of modern art. His technical skill with a brush remains nearly unsurpassed, even as we move into the twenty-first century. His themes and visions, his dreamscapes and Pandora's Box of nightmares still perplex and even shock today's art audiences. Even those who view Salvador Dali's art today are uncertain of his messages, however. They want to understand *what* he meant by his art. That, of course, is the wrong way to approach Salvador Dali.

His paintings had personal meaning for him, and his symbols all had homes in his Freudian-exposed unconscious, but it mattered little to this Spanish master whether anyone ever understood him or his paintings as he saw them. Instead, the legacy and genius of Dali remains in his hope that his audience would be driven not to interpret his dreams but to interpret their own. As one views a confused canvas portraying Dali's crutches; his human "drawers"; his floating cruciforms; his melting timepieces; his atom-powered altarpieces; his misshapened, grotesque anatomies; his Rocks of Cadaques; his Gala—the question is not What did Dali mean by it all? But rather, What do **you** see? What do **you** feel? What crawls under **your** skin? What lies under **your** bed, the place where **you** dream?

Chronology and Timeline

1904   Salvador Dali is born on May 11, in the town of Figueres, in Catalonia, Spain.

1908–10   Attends the Figueres Municipal Primary School.

1916–21   Attends the Figueres Institute and the Academy of the Marist Order.

1921   Attends the School of Painting, Sculpture, and Drawing, in Madrid; there he makes lifelong friends, including Luis Buñuel and Federico Garcia Lorca.

1922   After experimenting with cubism, Dali abandons the Picasso style and adopts the ideas of the Metaphysical School of painting; he is suspended from school for an alleged rebellious incident.

1924   Imprisoned for alleged political activity against the Spanish government.

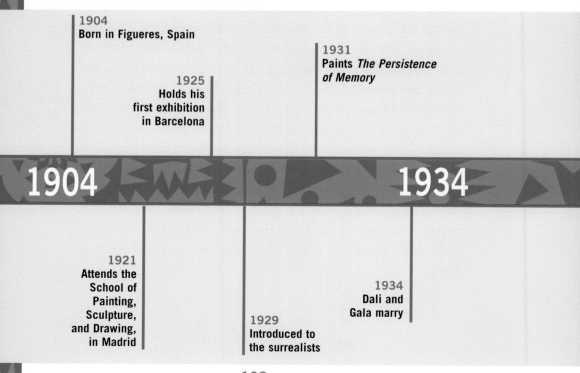

1904
Born in Figueres, Spain

1925
Holds his
first exhibition
in Barcelona

1931
Paints *The Persistence of Memory*

1904

1934

1921
Attends the
School of
Painting,
Sculpture,
and Drawing,
in Madrid

1929
Introduced to
the surrealists

1934
Dali and
Gala marry

1925 Returns to the School of Painting in Madrid, where he is influenced by the writings of Sigmund Freud; holds his first exhibition in Barcelona and meets Picasso.

1926 Expelled from the School of Painting; has his second solo exhibition at the Dalmau Gallery.

1928 Dali's first paintings, *Ana Maria* and *Seated Girl*, are shown in the United States.

1929 Visits Paris, where he is introduced to the surrealists, including André Breton and Paul Éluard; there he meets Gala, who becomes the love of his life; before year's end, his surrealist film *Un Chien Andalou* receives its first public showing.

1930 Illustrates Breton and Éluard's *The Immaculate Conception*; collaborates on a second surrealist film, *L'Age d'Or*

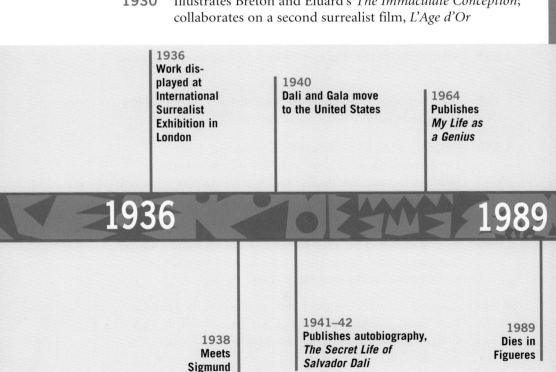

1936
Work displayed at International Surrealist Exhibition in London

1940
Dali and Gala move to the United States

1964
Publishes *My Life as a Genius*

1936

1989

1938
Meets Sigmund Freud

1941–42
Publishes autobiography, *The Secret Life of Salvador Dali*

1989
Dies in Figueres

(*The Golden Age*), with Buñuel; establishes his theory of the "paranoiac-critical method."

1931 Paints his famous *The Persistence of Memory*.

1932 Holds an exhibition at the Julien Levy Gallery, in New York City.

1933 Has his first solo exhibition at the Julien Levy Gallery.

1934 Holds his first solo exhibition in London, at the Zwemmer Gallery; surrealists criticize Dali for his alleged support of Hitler and right-wing politics; he and Gala marry in a civil ceremony; Dali leaves the surrealists' group and visits the United States for the first time.

1936 Participates in an exhibition at the International Surrealist Exhibition, London, where he delivers a lecture while dressed in a diving suit; Spanish Civil War drives Dali and Gala abroad; Edward James becomes his biggest patron.

1937 Visits Italy for the first time, where he studies Renaissance art.

1938 With help from Edward James and Stefan Zweig, Dali has the opportunity to meet Sigmund Freud.

1939 Creates a surrealist window for the Bonwit Teller Department Store in New York City—he accidentally smashes the window display and is arrested; Spanish Civil War ends with the rise to power of dictator General Francisco Franco.

1940 As World War II expands across Europe, Dali and Gala move to neutral Spain, then to the United States, where they remain for the next eight years.

1941–42 A major retrospective exhibition of Dali's work opens at New York's Museum of Modern Art, then travels to eight cities; Dali publishes his autobiography, *The Secret Life of Salvador Dali*.

1943	Creates illustrations for several published books.
1948	Salvador and Gala return to Spain from their eight-year exile in the United States; he illustrates *50 Secrets of Magic Craftsmanship*.
1949	Begins painting religious works; visits with Pope Pius XII for the first time.
1951–52	Paints *Christ of St. John of the Cross* and publishes *Manifesto Mystique* as a primer explaining his attraction to mysticism.
1954–55	Publishes a book on his mustache.
1955	Has his second audience with Pope Pius XII.
1958	Marries Gala in a church wedding.
1964	Publishes his book *My Life as a Genius*.
1974	Dali's Theater-Museum opens in his hometown of Figueres.
1975	Fascist dictator Francisco Franco dies, and Spain becomes a democracy.
1982	After a relationship that lasted for 53 years, Gala dies.
1989	Salvador Dali dies in Figueres, on January 23.

Notes

Chapter 1

1 Ian Gibson, *The Shameful Life of Salvador Dali* (New York: W.W. Norton & Company, 1997), 332.

Chapter 2

2 Paul Moorhouse, *Dali* (New York: Mallard Press, 1990), 6.
3 Robert Goff, *The Essential Salvador Dali* (New York: Harry N. Abrams, Inc., 1998), 14.
4 Gibson, 45.
5 Ibid., 47.
6 Kenneth Wach, *Salvador Dali: Masterpieces from the Collection of the Salvador Dali Museum* (New York: Harry N. Abrams, Inc., 1996), 8.
7 Gibson, 54.
8 Robert Anderson, *Salvador Dali* (Danbury, Conn.: Franklin Watts, 2002), 6.
9 Gibson, 57.
10 Moorhouse, 6.
11 Gibson, 64.
12 Ibid.
13 Ibid., 57.
14 Moorhouse, 6.
15 Ibid.
16 Gibson, 59.
17 Moorhouse, 6.
18 Gibson, 59.
19 Ibid., 60.
20 Ibid., 61.
21 Ibid., 65.
22 Ibid., 71.

Chapter 3

23 Ibid., 74.
24 Ibid., 75.
25 Ibid.
26 Ibid., 76.
27 Ibid., 78.
28 Moorhouse, 6.
29 Gibson, 79.
30 Ibid., 81.
31 Wach, 9.

32 Gibson, 86.
33 Ibid., 87.
34 Ibid., 91.
35 Moorhouse, 7.
36 Ibid.
37 Wach, 9.
38 Gibson, 103.
39 Wach, 10.
40 Ibid.
41 Gibson, 121.
42 Ibid., 73.
43 Anderson, 12.
44 Goff, 36.
45 Gibson, 520.

Chapter 4

46 Gibson, 20.
47 Goff, 20.
48 Ibid., 24.
49 Ibid., 22.
50 Wach, 12.
51 Goff, 36.
52 Anderson, 12.

Chapter 5

53 Gibson, 173.
54 Wach, 44.
55 Goff, 40.
56 Gibson, 243.
57 Ibid.
58 Goff, 43.
59 Ibid., 41.
60 Moorhouse, 9.
61 Ibid.
62 Goff, 45.
63 Gibson, 277.
64 Ibid.
65 Ibid., 282.
66 Ibid., 292.
67 Ibid., 293.
68 Anderson, 18.
69 Ibid.
70 Wach, 14.
71 Ibid.
72 Ibid.
73 Anderson, 19.

Chapter 6

74 Wach, 15.
75 Ibid.
76 Ibid., 16.
77 Ibid.
78 Ibid.
79 Ibid.
80 Ibid.
81 Moorhouse, 30.
82 Gibson, 263.
83 Ibid., 303.
84 Goff, 57.
85 Conroy Maddox, *Salvador Dali: Eccentric and Genius* (Cologne, West Germany: Benedikt Tschen Verlag GmbH & Co., 1990), 25.

Chapter 7

86 Gibson, 397.
87 Ibid., 397–98.
88 Goff, 62.
89 Ibid., 58.
90 Ibid.
91 Ibid., 64.
92 Gibson, 414.
93 Ibid., 437.
94 Ibid., 439.
95 Ibid., 438.
96 Ibid.

Chapter 8

97 Goff, 68.
98 Ibid., 70.
99 Ibid., 80.
100 Anderson, 33.
101 Goff, 82.
102 Ibid.
103 Gibson, 463.
104 Ibid., 489.
105 Ibid., 444.

Chapter 9

106 Goff, 96.
107 Ibid., 92.
108 Gibson, 497.
109 Ibid., 500.
110 Ibid., 501.
111 Goff, 96.
112 Ibid.
113 Ibid., 98.
114 Gibson, 642.
115 Goff, 110.
116 Anderson, 42.
117 Ibid.
118 Ibid.

Bibliography

Ades, Dawn. *Dali*. New York: Thames & Hudson Inc., 1995.

Anderson, Robert. *Salvador Dali*. Danbury, Conn.: Franklin Watts, 2002.

Finkelstein, Haim, ed. *The Collected Writings of Salvador Dali*. New York: Cambridge University Press, 1998.

Gibson, Ian. *The Shameful Life of Salvador Dali*. New York: W.W. Norton & Company, 1997.

Goff, Robert. *The Essential Salvador Dali*. New York: Harry N. Abrams, Inc., 1998.

Lubar, Robert S. *Dali*. New York: Little, Brown and Company, 1991.

Maddox, Conroy. *Salvador Dali: Eccentric and Genius*. Cologne, West Germany: Benedikt Tschen Verlag GmbH & Co., 1990.

Moorhouse, Paul. *Dali*. New York: Mallard Press, 1990.

Wach, Kenneth. *Salvador Dali: Masterpieces from the Collection of the Salvador Dali Museum*. New York: Harry N. Abrams, Inc., 1996.

Wenzel, Angela. *The Mad, Mad, Mad World of Salvador Dali*. New York: Prestel Verlag, 2003.

Web sites

Retrospective of Salvador Dali's Work
www.daliuniverse.com

Gala-Salvador Dali Foundation
www.dali-estate.org

Salvador Dali Art Gallery
www.dali-gallery.com

Dali Museum, St. Petersburg, Florida
www.salvadordalimuseum.org

The Museum of Modern Art, New York
www.moma.org

British and International Modern Art
www.tate.org.uk

Further Reading

Dali, Salvador, and Luis Romero. *Salvador Dali*. Barcelona: Ediciones Poligrafa S.A., 2004.

Etherington-Smith, Meredith. *The Persistence of Memory: A Biography of Dali*. Cambridge, Mass.: Da Capo Press, 1995.

Lubar, Robert S. *Dali: The Salvador Dali Museum Collection*. New York: Bullfinch Press 1994.

Pinchot, Antonio, Peter C. Sutton, and Eric Zaffran. *Dali's Optical Illusions*. New Haven, Conn.: Yale University Press, 1999.

Tush, Peter, and Michael Elsohn Ross. *Salvador Dali and the Surrealists: Their Lives and Ideas with 21 Activities*. Chicago, Ill.: Chicago Review Press, 2003.

Index

Picture Credits

About the Author

Tim McNeese is Associate Professor of History at York College, in York, Nebraska. Professor McNeese earned an Associate of Arts degree from York College, a Bachelor of Arts in History and Political Science from Harding University, and a Master of Arts in History from Southwest Missouri State University.

A prolific author of books for elementary, middle and high school, and college readers, McNeese has published more than 70 books and educational materials over the past 20 years, on everything from Western wagon trains to the Space Race. His writing has earned him a citation in the library reference work *Something about the Author*. He recently appeared as a consulting historian for the History Channel series *Risk Takers, History Makers*. His wife, Beverly, is Assistant Professor of English at York College. They have two children, Noah and Summer. Readers are encouraged to contact Professor McNeese at tdmcneese@york.edu.